Ontario Memories

Terry Boyle

—〜—

Polar Bear Press

First edition

distributed by
North 49 Books
35 Prince Andrew Place
Toronto, Ontario M3C 2H2
(416) 449-4000

Canadian Cataloguing in Publication Data

Boyle, Terry
      Ontario Memories

Rev. ed.
Previously published under title: Memories of Ontario
Includes bibliographical references and index.
ISBN 1-896757-06-5

I. Ontario – History, Local   I. Title   II. Title: Memories of Ontario

FC3061.B69 1998   971.3   C98-930821-9
F1057.B69 1998

Printed in Canada

Ontario Memories

PREFACE

The arrival of the Loyalists in Canada changed the shape of the country. Prior to their arrival, most of the settlers had been French; this influx created two different cultural groups in Canada. The French-Canadians held their farms under the seigneurs; the Loyalists wanted to own their farms outright, as they had done in the Thirteen Colonies.

The Loyalists felt their settlements were too far away from the governor of Quebec and they wanted their own government. Few Loyalists had settled in present-day Quebec and this made it possible for Parliament in Great Britain to attempt to please both the English and the French. Canada was divided into two separate provinces. This division took place under the Canada Act of 1791, and the Ottawa River formed the boundary. The western province, which was predominantly English-speaking, was called Upper Canada; the eastern province, which was predominantly French-speaking was called Lower Canada. A governor was appointed for the whole of Canada and a lieutenant-governor for each province.

The first lieutenant-governor of Upper Canada was Colonel John Graves Simcoe. The governor foresaw that Upper Canada would one day become a great province. His wife accompanied him on his travels and her skillful sketches and her detailed diary reveal life and land in Upper Canada in those early days.

Memories of Ontario is an historical outline of the unfolding of the province of Ontario. It is meant to reveal to the reader the vision of our fore-fathers and the common spirit behind the vision of our individual towns and cities. Instead of a myriad of details I hope it will invoke your love, curiosity, interest, awareness, humour, surprise and a host of other feelings for this, our homeland. I hope to show you the variety of heritages that have blended in the province — the names, the cultural gifts, the knowledge and the directions.

Memories of Ontario can put you in your car and set you on a journey of discovery. It can take you to adventures unthought-of and give meaning to things previously unnoticed and probably things taken very much for granted. I hope this book awakens your interest to many new things in Ontario.

Terry Boyle

―――――――――――

CONTENTS

❂ ❂ ❂

❦ ❦ ❦

Dedication

To the memory of Delores Victor,
who believed that all people had creative potential
and were capable of fulfilling their dreams.

Special thanks to

Lana, Sarah, Jeremy and Two Bears

ACTON

Workers repairing the main street of Acton.

The town of Acton is the most northerly town in Halton County, situated at the junction of Highway 7 and 25. Many people today identify Acton with its large leather industry, a far cry from 1829, when the site was known only as four hundred acres on the 2nd and 3rd Concessions of Esquesing.

The first settlers to arrive were Zenas, Rufus, and Ezra Adams. In the first dry goods store operated by Wheeler Green, a young man called Dan was employed. Young Dan must have been an up-and-coming fellow, since, for some unexplained reason, the settlement was named after him, Danville. Later the name would change to Adamsville, in honour of the first settlers and in 1844, Robert Swan, the first postmaster there, named the village Acton after his hometown in Northumberland, England.

Acton quickly became the centre of a farming community and the first industry was a grist mill. By 1837 the first tannery was set up in a forest clearing and was operated by Abraham Nelles. Although the tannery changed hands several times, it was obviously here to stay. In 1865, the Breadmore Company took over the operation and expanded until it became Acton's major industry.

Other industries located in Acton during its early days were J.H. Coates stave and barrel factory, W.H. Storey's glove factory, Browns and Halls lumber and shingle mill, Speight's blacksmith and carriage works and Acton's famous Plow Manufacturing Company. There was also a lime works that went into operation in 1872 with two kilns capable of burning 350 bushels of lime a day. Acton was also well supplied with stores, hotels, livery stables and bakeshops. It flourished!

As the pioneer population increased, so did various religious groups. Ministers of all the churches served their people faithfully, but one, the Reverend D.B. Cameron, left behind him a somewhat unique bequest. He had ministered to the Presbyterians in Acton from 1875 to 1885. On February 25, 1890, at the age of 73, he died at the home of Peter Mann. And he left a will!

Cameron was a native of Inverness, Scotland and was known as a man of high ideals. He believed in the simple life as was obvious from his will. It read, "Considering the foolish extravagance displayed by the community in general and as a protest against it (I almost believe a solitary protest), I direct that my body, when dead, shall be decently wrapped in bleached cotton, neatly prepared for the purpose, laid in a simple coffin made of pine, with no ornamentation not so much as my name, and carried to the grave in a sleigh, if in winter, or a spring wagon and laid in the grave without a shell; and that no monument of any kind be put to mark the place unless some friend take a boulder from the field to mark the spot, and, if he fancy to do so, cut thereon the initials D.B.C."

Acton was incorporated as a village in 1873. On October 1, 1968, the town of Acton annexed part of Esquesing Township. On January 1, 1974 Acton was amalgamated with the town of Georgetown and they became the Town of Halton Hills.

Driving through today, the town seems to have remained somewhat untouched by progress. The main street, except for different signs on the storefronts, seems relatively unchanged. Period homes, and hundred-year-old maples landscape most of Acton's streets. At the Olde Hide House one can peruse a tremendous selection of leather garments and furs.

Other attractions for the general public include Canadian furniture, knitted goods and ceramics; other industries include electronic manufacturing, plastics and tools.

From Danville to Halton Hills is a trip in years, not miles, with many landmarks visible from each period of time.

AMHERSTBURG

Young boys taking a break from working on a dirt street in Amherstburg.

The history of Amherstburg dates back to the days of French rule in the 1730's. In those days the French lived and traded among the Wyandot or Huron nation. The native people had long occupied this area. On August 11, 1679, Robert Cavalier, sieur de La Salle, sailed his little barque, the Griffin, up the Detroit River. The official recorder of the voyage, Father Louis Hennepin, a Rocollet priest wrote," The Banks are vast meadows and the prospect is terminated with some hills covered with vineyards, trees bearing fruit, groves and forest, so well disposed that one would think that Nature alone could not have made, without the help of Art, so charming a prospect." He continued to praise the natives' carefully tended gardens, their neat rows of beans, melons, pumpkins, corn and tobacco. Through the trees were the longhouses, placed at intervals along the Indian trail that was destined to be, in the future, Highway 8.

During the American Revolution, an influx of Loyalists took up land grants near the present site of Amherstburg. Lieutenant-Colonel William Caldwell, who had served with Butler's Rangers at Niagara and Detroit, and Colonel Matthew Elliot, who later became deputy superintendent of the Indian Department, both located here in 1784.

The construction of Fort Malden began in 1797 by the Second

A photograph showing what Fort Malden looked like in 1895.

Battalion of the Royal Canadian Volunteers. This replaced a military post at Detroit that had been evacuated by the British in 1796 under the terms of the Jay Treaty. The town of Amherstburg came into being during this period when a portion of the military reserve was laid out as a town site. The military settlement was named after Lord Jeffery Amherst, Governor-General of British North America from 1760-63. Situated on the east bank of the Detroit River near its junction with Lake Erie this settlement was destined to be involved in the War of 1812 with the United States. Work commenced at Fort Malden to reinforce it against an American invasion. It was here that General Isaac Brock and Tecumseh, the great Shawnee Chief, met at two o'clock in the morning to discuss a plan for the attack on Detroit. Tecumseh and his men had fought the Americans before. In one fight, Tecumseh and seventy of his followers were able to trap a force of two hundred American soldiers on horseback. Tecumseh had planned the attack so well that more than half of the Americans were wiped out and yet only one of his warriors died.

Tecumseh disliked the Americans and he feared them as much as the British. The Shawnee and the neighbouring tribes were worried about losing their home. During the War of 1812, other native peoples, like the Wyandot's, also joined forces with Britain. Thanks to the native alliance, the Americans lost the war and Canada remained intact.

General Brock and Tecumseh spent most of that August night in council. The plan was a good one – almost as soon as the attack began on Detroit, General Hull of the American forces surrendered. Three days later General Brock and Tecumseh were sitting together in Fort Detroit.

Meanwhile, in the navy yard near Fort Malden, ships were under construction to increase the British naval force. It was 1813, when the British fleet suffered defeat in the Battle of Lake Erie. The troops were ordered to retreat from Fort Malden and Detroit and all public buildings were burned. Not until the year 1815, under the terms of the Treaty of Ghent, was the fort restored to the British.

During the Upper Canada Rebellion of 1837-38, Amherstburg was the scene of military action once more. The garrison of Fort Malden and the local militia repelled four attempts by supporters of William Lyon Mackenzie to invade Upper Canada on the Detroit River frontier.

Fort Malden remained a British garrison until 1851, when the Imperial troops were withdrawn and the fort was occupied only by military pensioners. That same year Amherstburg was incorporated as a village. In 1859, Fort Malden was abandoned by the military. By the end of 1878, Amherstburg was a town.

For the Wyandot Indians, the influx of Loyalists to the region eventually forced them to surrender their lands and move to a reserve. By the 1830's their old council house had collapsed. In the 1870's their reserve was auctioned off and the remaining Wyandots, possibly one hundred, were forced to assimilate into the white world.

The town of Amherstburg continued to thrive as a mercantile and manufacturing centre and to retain its historical atmosphere. In the older section of town, the streets are narrow and the houses, as old as the early 1800's, front directly on the sidewalks. The Anglican Church, built in 1819, on land donated by Colonel William Caldwell, is one of the oldest churches in western Ontario. Amherstburg has a very old cemetery with a monument nearby to honour those who fell in the War of 1812. Fort Malden is now part of a National historic park. Several stone buildings house mementoes of the native peoples, the French, the British, and the Americans who contributed to various aspects of the history of the area. The park contains part of the 1796 British earthworks of the fort and reflects Amherstburg as a military community at one time.

The North American Black Historical Museum in Amherstburg helps to preserve the heritage of the black people – from their origins in Africa and experiences of slavery to their emancipation and settlement in this area. Amherstburg played a vital role during the years of slavery in the United States. This settlement was a key centre on the road to freedom for black people through the Underground Railroad. For the oppressed black people, Amherstburg was a refuge of safety and freedom.

Amherstburg is a classic settlement that readily reveals its colourful military, Indian and black history. Most aspects of the varied cultural past we have in Ontario can be found in this small town. Despite its modern business establishments and factories this town of about 6,000 people retains its historic atmosphere.

BARRIE

The Barrie Market Building after the renovations of 1877.

The founder of Barrie was an agent of the Hudson's Bay Company, although his name has been lost to history. It is said that he came across the sheltered bay on the west coast of Lake Simcoe and went ashore. The layout of the land impressed him so strongly that shortly after, in 1812, a Hudson Bay Company storehouse was built on this site.

The building once stood only a few yards west of the railway depot, near the old landing place. It was here that the southwestern terminus of a trail known as the Nine-Mile Portage, led to Willow Creek and on to the open waters of Georgian Bay by canoe down the Nottawasaga River.

The Portage route had already been established by the native population prior to the 1800's. From 1812-1815, the trail was widened to accommodate sleighs and wagons on their way to government posts of the Upper Great Lakes, posts such as Fort Michilimacinac at the entrance to Lake Michigan. Many of the major roadways today were once portage routes or overland trails used by native people.

The settlement of Kempenfelt, situated three miles east of the head of the Bay and now part of Barrie proper, gained some importance during the War of 1812. The hamlet was a link when the Portage route functioned as a military route, between Lake Simcoe and Lake Huron. The government built military storehouses at either end of the Portage. The storehouse at the head of the Bay served as a stop-over for traders and settlers bound for neighbouring townships. This military post on Lake Simcoe was protected and it was supplied for a few years by an armed schooner that was stationed at Holland Landing.

The first log dwelling on the site of the present city of Barrie was built by French Canadians serving under Sir George Head. He had been sent to Canada in 1815 to supervise a proposed naval establishment at Penetanguishene and chose to reside at the head of the Bay.

Andrew Borland, a trader, patented part of the town site of Barrie, on March 9th, 1827. This parcel of land became known later as the Berczy Block in Barrie. The government buildings on Marks Street were situated on a military reserve of forty-five acres, bounded on the west by Bayfield Street and on the east by Berczy Street. By 1830, the government disposed of the reserve to Captain Oliver, but at the end of two years for some reason, the Captain sold it back to the government, who, in turn, surveyed it into lots. The town received its name from Commodore Barrie, British Warship Commander at Kingston during the early 1800's.

By the spring of 1832, the government built shanties along Dunlop street for settlers. One early settler who arrived during this time was Alexander Walker, a farmer of Scottish descent who had taken unto himself as a wife, Miss Betsy Sweezy, of Holland Landing. Their housekeeping experience in Barrie was in a dwelling which resembled a barn; indeed, the building was afterwards used as a barn. In June 1830, a party of visitors from Yonge Street called upon the Walkers in their primitive dwelling and, although strangers, were invited to share a meal. To their surprise, the main dish was a homemade cake baked outdoors in the ashes of the fire kept burning in the yard for domestic purposes. Such were Barrie's beginnings.

Two log taverns were erected in 1832, and a general store was built the same year. Dr. Archibald Pass, the first doctor in Barrie, arrived in 1835. The post office opened in 1835 and a schoolhouse the following year. By 1851, Barrie had a population of 800 and was incorporated as a town without any municipal organization.

The Ontario, Simcoe and Huron Railway was built from Toronto to Collingwood during the 1850's, and it passed through Allandale, one mile from Barrie. According to some accounts, the reason the railway bypassed Barrie was the refusal on the part of the community to grant a

The Northern Railway Station in Barrie c. 1875.

bonus to the railway. The chief engineer has been quoted to say, "I will make grass grow in Barrie's Streets and pave Allandale's streets with gold". A more plausible reason for locating the train station at Allandale instead of Barrie was the engineering problem presented by the hills surrounding the town. Eventually the railway was extended into Barrie and it provided the key to prosperity. Allandale lost its identity when it was amalgamated with Barrie in 1897.

Today, the Barrie city hall stands on the same site where, in 1843, the first market building had been erected. Additions were made to the front of the building in 1856 and to the back in 1873. A mansard roof was added in 1885. Work began in 1946 to drastically remodel the building. The ornamental ironwork and the tops of the towers were removed, as well as the mansard roof and the chimneys. The two-storey building was changed to a three- storey structure, to house the municipal offices.

Barrie, population of 20,279, was incorporated on January 1, 1959, as a city. At the same time Barrie annexed an additional area of 2,537 acres of land. The city fathers resolved to adopt as their slogan: "Beautiful Barrie, Ontario's Most Progressive City". In 1964, another 1,752 acres from Vespra Township were annexed.

If one single development could symbolize the great post-war recreational invasion and economic development of Simcoe County it would be the construction of Highway 400 from Toronto to a little north of Barrie. It has been called "Ontario's Vacationland Freeway". It was the first four-lane highway in Ontario. It was started in 1945 and took three years to complete. In the mid-1960's a two-lane extension was added north of Barrie to join Highway 103 at Coldwater. By 1970 plans were announced to widen the existing highway to six lanes. This work was finished in 1972.

Prior to the building of Highway 400, the population of Barrie had only increased from 6,024 in 1901 to 10,633 in 1945. Although the building of Highway 400 was important for all of Simcoe County, the greatest impact was felt in Barrie. The community was less than one hour from Toronto and was the gateway to the north. A new commuter city, for the greater city of Toronto, had been born.

A city alive with entertainment and recreational opportunities on Lake Simcoe's Kempenfelt Bay, Barrie is known as the site of North America's largest annual dog show. Every year a winter carnival is held on the frozen waters of Kempenfelt Bay, and it attracts thousands of visitors to a place many call the "Capital of Huronia". Horse fans arrive every Wednesday and Saturday to watch harness racing at the fair grounds of the Barrie Raceway. The Base Borden Military Museum hosts an outdoor exhibit displaying an amazing array of military hardware and memorabilia. Molsen Park, a 240 acre entertainment site, offers an on-going series of major annual attractions ranging from musical concerts to sports events.

History buffs would enjoy visiting the County Museum and Archives located eight kilometres outside of Barrie on Hwy. 26. The complex consists of several period buildings and a modern display centre, with a replica of shops from 1840. The museum traces the history of man in the area from 5,000 B.C. to present day. Especially impressive is the native exhibition.

Barrie has the quality of two jewels set in one ring: one reflects the new age of development with a main street bordered by endless restaurants and a shopping mall, the other reflects nature's beauty.

BRAMPTON

The main street of Brampton.

The Flower City, Brampton, situated in the valley of the Etobicoke River, dates back to the 1820's. Surveyors of the time described the area as low and swampy and covered with dense hardwood forest, but this description did not deter the early settlers, who were predominatly of British origin, from establishing settlement here.

Samuel Kenny, the first landowner to arrive, later sold his property to John Elliot, a native of Brampton, England. John Elliot quickly cleared and laid out his property into village lots and named the community after his former home.

Martin Salisbury opened a tavern in 1822, on the high ground at the north end of Main Street. Another tavern was erected by a Mr. Buffy and stood at the Main and Queen Street intersection. The early settlement grew around these two taverns. Saddlebag preachers held services here and farmers came to discuss the business of the day. Soon visiting magistrats from York came and held court in one of the taverns.

Two leading citizens, John Elliot and John Scott were responsible for laying the foundations for the future development of Brampton. They established a distillery, a cooperage, and a potasher, thus setting the industrial wheels in motion.

In 1845, a great influx of Irish immigrants arrived in Canada and many settled in Brampton. By 1852, the hamlet was large enough to be incorporated as a village. Brampton was, by then, spread out on both sides of the Etobicoke Creek and connected by three bridges. There were seven churches including three Methodist. John Elliot and a friend, by the name of William Lawson, were instrumental in creating a centre here for Primitive Methodism in Upper Canada.

The Grand Trunk Railway arrived in the village in 1858, providing a forward thrust in the form of two large industries: the Haggart Foundry manufactured farm machinery and stoves, and the Dale Estate Nurseries became famous for the propagation of hybrid roses and orchids. Many more nurseries arrived in later years to become the largest employers in the community until the 1940's. The presence of this large garden industry gave Brampton its title, "Flower City". Brampton in the 1860's became the County Town. In 1867, a courthouse was built to serve the county at a cost of $40,000.

Until the 1940's the population figure for Brampton remained fairly static. The town was a centre for the rich farming area that surrounded it and there was sufficient light industry to make for a balanced economy. Since the end of World War Two, the character of Brampton has been undergoing change. New industries have moved to the area and a variety of goods, from shoes and furnaces to communications equipment and automobiles, are manufactured here. Shopping and recreational facilities have been enlarged and Brampton now has one of the largest shopping malls outside the greater Toronto area.

The preservation of history is certainly reflected throughout the City of Brampton. The Great Flying Museum located just north of Brampton exhibits armaments, instruments, a machine gun periscope and other memorabilia of World War One. The museum also features flying aircraft including a Fokker D7, a Dr1 (tri- plane), and SE5A biplane.

The Peel Heritage Complex situated on Wellington Street represents the heritage of Peel Region. In this renovated 19th century Peel County Jail and adjacent Registry Office, the regional museum, archives and art gallery have been brought together.

BRANTFORD

Seven of the oldest Chiefs of the Six Nations, c. 1900.

Joseph Brant gave the city of Brantford its name. Also known as Tyenandaga, this man was the great Mohawk War Chief who led the Six Nations people to the banks of the Grand River in 1784, after the close of the American Revolution. The site was, at that time, known as Brant's Ford.

General Haldimand granted a large portion of land, a strip six miles wide on either side of the entire length of the Grand River (165 miles), to the Mohawk nation who had supported the British during the revolution. Much of the Mohawk grant was later sold by the Mohawks to incoming white settlers.

Joseph Brant was born on the banks of the Ohio River in 1742. He received his education in Lebanon, Connecticut, at Moor's Indian Charity School. He later became Chief Tyenandaga of his Mohawk tribe. He first joined forces with the English during the French-Indian War and in 1763 fought with the Iroquois against Pontiac. He later devoted himself to missionary work and translated the Prayer Book and St. Mark's Gospel into the Mohawk tongue in 1787. When Guy Johnson was named superintendent of Indian Affairs in 1774, Brant served as his secretary. At the outbreak of the American Revolution, Joseph Brant remained pro-British and organized and led the Mohawk people and other tribes, who were allied to the British against the settlements on the New York frontier. After the war he discouraged the continuance of Indian warfare and aided the commissioners of the United States in securing treaties of peace with the Miamis and other western tribes. In Upper Canada he settled down and devoted himself to missionary work.

On the outskirts of present day Brantford, the people of the Six Nations built a village and remained at peace. In 1785, by order of King George the Third of England, a chapel was built for the native people. Royal assent was given in 1904, to call it "His Majesty's Chapel of the Mohawk". It is, today, the oldest Protestant church in Ontario.

In 1805, John Stalts, a man of white and native blood, built a log hut on the high bank of the river. By the 1820's three trading stores were opened by John A. Wilkes, S.V. Douglas and Nathan Gage. A few mills were erected, but settlement remained at a standstill until the town site of Brantford was surrendered to the crown by the Mohawks in 1830. That year Lewis Burwell arrived and surveyed the site and laid out the lots for settlement. By public auction on May 14, 1831, lots were sold on Colborne Street to the following settlers: James Cockshutt, W. Spencer, James Durand, Abraham Cook, John Benjamin, James Torm and others. On Dalhousie Street, the purchasers were James Gilpin, John Mitchell, W.F. Whitehead, C. Austin, A. Richardson and John Cunningham.

Rufus Houghton built the first tannery and two hotels and a distillery came into being through the efforts of John Lovejoy and John A. Wilkes. William Spencer opened the first brewery shortly thereafter.

When, in 1840, the Grand River Navigation Company built a canal linking Brantford to Lake Erie by water, the village increased substantially. By this time Brantford had a population of 3,000 and its own municipal government. On July 28, 1847, it was incorporated as a town and two years later the town hall was erected on the Market Square. When the railway arrived, the town became the distributing centre for one of the richest agricultural areas in Western Ontario.

Brantford proudly calls itself "Telephone City", as it was at Tutela Heights, just outside the city, that Alexander Graham Bell invented the telephone in the summer of 1875.

Detail of a bronze bas-relief depicting a War Council on Joseph Brant's monument in Brantford.

Alexander Graham Bell was born in Edinburgh, Scotland in 1847. He received his education at the universities of Edinburgh and London. After the death of his two brothers, the family immigrated in 1870 to settle in Brantford, Ontario.

Bell went to Massachusetts the following year where he taught visible speech, opened a school for teachers of the deaf, and in 1873 became a professor of vocal physiology at Boston University.

At this time, Thomas Sanders and G.G. Hubbard, whose children were receiving instruction from Bell, learned of his experiments on electrical devices to teach speech and offered to finance him. With their help, Bell went ahead with his experiments and in 1875, he and his assistant, Thomas A. Watson, sent tones and overtones over wire. The following year they transmitted the first intelligible sentence. Alexander Bell's telephone patent was issued on March 7, 1876. In 1877, he formed the Bell Telephone Company, American Telephone and Telegraph Company.

Bell also invented the photophone that carries sound on a beam of light and devised an apparatus to locate metal objects in the human body. Alexander Bell's accomplishments continued over the course of his life to include the development of the iron lung for artificial respiration and a method of locating icebergs by echo. In later years he served as president of the National Geographic Society from 1894 to 1904. Bell passed away in 1922.

Brantford entrepreneurs and industrialists have made large contributions to the city's growth. It was here on a farm outside the city that

Alanson Harris produced the first Canadian-designed farm machine. This man helped to lay the foundation for the world-renowned Massey Ferguson Company. The city today is a centre of farm machinery manufacturing and is known as the "Combine Capital of the World". Brantford's large industries are manufacturers of iron, steel and paper products, electrical fittings, motor trucks, refrigerators, waxes, varnishes, textiles and clothing. It is also served by a municipal airport.

Today, the Bell homestead in Brantford is preserved as a National Historic site. The home of the Reverend Thomas Henderson, who served as the first General Agent for the telephone company, was moved in 1969 to a site adjacent to the Bell home.

The Brant County Museum, located in Brantford, features a fine Six Nations Indian collection and the life histories of Captain Joseph Brant and Pauline Johnson, poetess and writer.

Anyone interested in exploring the colourful history and cultures of the native peoples of Eastern Canada should visit the Woodland Indian Educational Centre and Museum.

Brantford, with its rich historical background and its many places of interest to the visitor, is well worth a stop-over on route 403.

BRONTE

Some say the mouth of the Twelve Mile Creek, running through the village of Bronte, is haunted. Once the site of the sacred hunting grounds of the Mississaugas, this spot of land remains cloaked in Indian Medicine. Many have claimed to have seen a Mississauga Indian Chief riding a white stallion.

Where a lone teepee once stood, a village grew named Bronte. One of the earliest settlers was Philip Sovereign and his family of German descent, who arrived in the area from Sussex County, New York, in 1814, and settled along Lake Ontario to the west of Twelve Mile Creek. He was followed by John Belyea, a United Empire Loyalist from New Brunswick who took up land to the east of the creek.

By 1833, a townsite was surveyed by William Hawkins and lots were offered for sale ranging to ten acres in size. A year later the village was referred to as Bronte, named in tribute to the British naval hero Horatio Nelson, one of whose titles was the Duke of Bronte.

With the construction of harbour facilities during the 1840's, Bronte progressed rapidly. By 1850, the village had two hundred inhabitants, two hotels, a sawmill, two grist mills, a clothing factory, a shingle mill, a wagon and blacksmith shop. On the east bank between Ontario Street and Lakeshore Road, The Bronte Steam Mills, a three-storey building and the largest in the province towered over the harbour. In 1856, Bronte's population had risen to 550. The quantity of grain being exported would soon reach some 300,000 bushels bound for England and New York State.

Schooners were also being built at Bronte. The largest ship built on The Twelve was the Peerless, a 172 ton vessel launched in 1853.

When the grain market collapsed in Upper Canada in the late 1850's, it was not surprising that Bronte turned to commercial fishing. The population of the village dropped from 550 to 200 during this period. The main catch had been whitefish and lake trout. In the following years the yellowback, or cisco, and a type of herring called the blueback became the major source of income. Where the grain warehouses had lined The Twelve, fishing shanties now stood.

Another form of income for Bronte was the stonehooking fleet. Using long-handled, two pronged rakes and working from a scow, the crew would pry loose strips of Dundas shale from the lake bottom. The stone was used in local construction and marketed in Toronto. At one time some 110 stonehookers operated out of Bronte harbour.

Bronte continued as a small settlement. By 1904, the population had only reached a total of 400 inhabitants. Even when Bronte was incorporated as a village in 1952, the citizens remained concerned about its rate of growth. On January 1, 1962, the Township of Trafalgar, The Town of Oakville and the village of Bronte were amalgamated into the Town of Oakville. At this time Bronte became a residential suburb of Oakville.

Pleasure boating is big business there today and many who have located in the area chose to do so for the excellent harbour facilities and access to Lake Ontario.

The original, natural beauty of the mouth of The Twelve is somewhat crowded by yachts and buildings but the magic and charm are still there.

BURLINGTON

Sons of England float in a parade marking the Coronation of King Edward VII.

The sandcliffs on the north shore of the bay looked like red rocks. The beach was like a park covered with large, spreading oaks. The bay was full of canoes, with Indians fishing for salmon. This was the scene witnessed in 1776, by Mrs. John Graves Simcoe, the wife of Governor Simcoe.

In the topographical description of Upper Canada, issued in London, in 1813, under the authority of Sir Frances Gore, the Burlington area is referred to 'perhaps as beautiful and romantic a situation as any in the interior of America'.

In the early beginnings of Burlington, Iroquois Chief Joseph Brant received a land grant of 3,450 acres overlooking Burlington Bay in the year 1784 for his services during the American Revolutionary War. He built a magnificent frame home by the bay and beachstrip. James Buchanan, British Consul in New York, described the home after a visit in 1819, "The house of Mr. Brant is on the shores of Lake Ontario, has noble and commanding aspect and stands on a spot of great natural beauty. We entered the door into the spacious hall, then proceeded into the parlour. It was a room well furnished with a carpet, pier, and chimney glasses, mahogony tables, fashionable chairs, a guitar, a neat hanging book-case in which among other volumes were perceived a Church of England Prayer Book translated into the Mohawk tongue." A room at the

Brant Inn as it appeared in 1910.

Brant Museum has been laid out in similar fashion. The museum, a replica of the Brant house, was built in 1937 to replace the original building, parts of which stood as recently as 1927.

In the early 1800's Brant sold some of his land to Loyalist friends. The first to settle on the present site of Burlington was August Bates, who arrived in 1800. Soon a community grew around Brant's home. After Joseph Brant's death on the 24th of November 1807, at age 64, James Gage of Stoney Creek, a friend of Brant's, purchased over 338 acres of land from the estate and laid out a townsite. He erected a mill and other commercial establishments.

By 1817, sixteen buildings now stood in the hamlet, which was orginally named Wellington Square in honour of the Duke of Wellington. In 1837, twenty wooden houses marked the beginning of this bustling centre. Soon wharves were constructed and a warehouse built along with a large steam flour mill. Wellington Square quickly became the headquarters for grain growers of the area. During this period Brant Street and Guelph Line were the two main roads providing access to the lake. Located at the bottom of each road were docks and warehouses. Wellington Square existed at the bottom of Brant and a small community named Port Nelson was established at the end of Guelph Line. Port Nelson was a small centre of docks and warehouses with two tall pines over one hundred feet high serving as landmarks for sailors.

Since the ice age had left a legacy of fertile soil on the plains around Lake Ontario, market gardening thrived as an industry. At times, farm

Lawn bowling at the Brant Inn in 1912.

wagons, laden with grain and produce, were lined up all the way from the lakeshore to Middle Road (Queen Elizabeth Highway) waiting to be shipped to the dozens of schooners anchored in the harbour. In 1844, almost 11,000 barrels of flour were shipped from the three docks at Wellington Square.

Many enterprising individuals started up in shipbuilding. One of the early shipbuilders of Wellington Square was Willet Green Miller. The lumber industry thrived for awhile, with seventeen sawmills operating in the community as early as 1846.

Wellington Square by the mid-nineteenth century had a tannery, a potter, two wagon makers, a foundry and several stores. William Button operated a brick shop at the foot of Brant Street and James Allen had started a carriage factory, to name just a couple of entrepreneurs.

Religion to the early settlers was a must. Prior to the 1830's, the pioneers of Wellington Square had various missionaries. St. Luke's Anglican Church was built in 1834, thanks to Elizabeth Brant, daughter of Chief Brant. She had solicited the necessary funds in England to build this church. She, her husband and son are buried in the churchyard.

Often the development of any one community reflects the hard work of a few families who prospered in servicing the settlement and returned some of their wealth for the benefit of all. One such Burlington family was the Fisher's.

The Fisher story begins in 1799, when a group of twenty families, all related by marriage, set out from Pennsylvania for Upper Canada.

Herman Fisher and his wife Mary Cline, were part of the group. Their son Peter was born in 1802, near Vineland.

When Herman died, Peter ventured to Wellington Square and purchased a large block of land between Middle Road and Prospect Street, extending east from the Guelph Line. There he cleared twelve acres of land, built a log cabin and married Sarah Bray. Sarah died in 1839, leaving Peter to tend five children. Peter married twice more and was father of ten children, the youngest born when he was fifty-four.

In 1837, he constructed a home called Shady Cottage with walls two feet thick and sixteen inch wide slabs of pine for flooring. The home remained in the Fisher family until it was demolished in 1968 for the development of the Burlington Mall on Guelph Line. Peter also donated an acre of land at the corner of his property for a twenty-four foot log schoolhouse.

Peter's son William inherited the farm after his death. William continued to plant more orchards and added forty more cows to their herd. Fisher's Dairy supplied milk for the entire town. At the turn of the century Fisher's Farms boasted 2,000 apple trees, 3,000 pear trees, 2,00 plum trees, 200 cherry trees, 100 peach trees, 300 grapevines, eight acres of strawberries and raspberries and five acres of red and black currants. Peter's great-grandson still operates Fisher's Farms now situated on Highway 5.

In 1873, the hamlets of Wellington Square and Port Nelson amalgamated and incorporated as the village of Burlington. The name Burlington is a corruption of Bridlington, a town in Yorkshire, England. At the time of incorporation the village numbered 750 inhabitants.

One of the earliest tourist attractions in Burlington was the Brant Inn located on Lake Ontario near Joseph Brant's home. Built in 1875, it offered easy access to sandy beaches and water sports. Acres of gardens and croquet and lawn bowling greens were available to the tourist. The Inn had a spacious ballroom where on many a night, locals and visitors danced the night away. The Brant Inn remained open until the 1970's.

By 1913, the village had annexed some of the adjoining territories and grown to a point that it could call itself a town in December of 1914. For the next forty years Burlington was primarily a centre for farm marketing. In 1958 the amalgamation of Burlington, Nelson Township and a part of East Flamborough Township created the new, larger town of Burlington. Farms disappeared and residential districts increased. Executives from Hamilton and other prosperous areas built elaborate homes in Burlington. A drive today, through the Roselawn district, east of Guelph Line by Lakeshore Road, tells it all.

By the end of 1958 the Burlington Bay Skyway was opened. This was the largest bridge ever built by the Ontario Department of Highways to that date. The centre span of the bridge is 120 feet above the harbour entrance and it is 4.37 miles long.

In the last decade Burlington has become a large manufacturing centre with upward of 140 manufacturing, distributing, and service companies.

Travelling down Brant Street today, the tourist can still see many period buildings, such as the Coronation and Sherwood Hotels, near the lake. A lovely shopping complex, resembling 18th century architecture, located to the east of Brant Street near the firehall, called Wellington Square deserves a visit. The wharves that once stood at the bottom of Brant Street no longer exist. Few would now know that the parkland along the Burlington lakefront was once covered by water where boats anchored behind the protection of the breakwall. To stand at the bottom of Brant or Guelph Line today, it is difficult to feel the awe that Lady Simcoe felt as the romantic scene that once was is not obscured by buildings.

CAMBRIDGE

The city of Cambridge has roots tapped into three towns. In 1973, the towns of Hespeler and Preston in Waterloo Township, and the city of Galt in North Dumfries were almagamated to become Cambridge. The name Cambridge was selected to commemorate the early name of the settlement at Preston.

First settled by John Erb in the early 1800's, Preston was the first root, four miles northwest of Galt on the Speed River near its confluence with the Grand River. The setttlement which sprang up became known as Erb's Mills and later Cambridge. The name Preston was introduced in 1830 at the suggestion of Squire Scollick, a prominent settler who originally came from Preston, England.

The local livery stable at Cambridge.

Soon after the name changed, warm mineral springs, sulphur springs, to be precise, were discovered at Preston by Peter Erb. An entrepreneur by the name of Samuel Cornell saw business potential in these sulphur springs and constructed a hotel nearby. Preston gained fame as a health spa. This hotel is believed by many to have been the first in Upper Canada to offer a bath with running water.

Preston in the 1850's hosted two grist mills, two sawmills, two vinegar factories, a woollen factory, a chair factory, two tanneries, a pottery, a starch factory, and three breweries. There were also many grand homes built in the old German style by inhabitants of German extraction.

In 1852, with a population of just over 1400, Preston was incorporated as a village; by 1899, it was a town.

During the first half of the 20th century, the population of Preston swelled to over 14,000. The many and diversified industries of the town included flour mills, stove factories, woollen mills, furniture factories and woodworking machinery plants. Preston was ready to apply for city status in the late 1960's but action to this effect was postponed.

The second root town of the city of Cambridge is Hespeler. This townsite was originally part of a crown grant given to the Six Nations Indians in recognition of their loyality to King George the Third during the American Revolutionary War. Richard Beasley of Hamilton who had bought a large tract of this land from the native people, sold 515 acres in 1818 to Abraham Clemens, a Loyalist from Pennsylvania.

Settlement did not begin in earnest until the 1830's when Michael Bergey built a log cabin in what later became the business centre of the town. At first, the place was called Bergeytown and, in 1835, the hamlet was renamed New Hope.

Jacob Hespeler, a native of Baden Germany, lived and prospered for a number of years in nearby Preston. He bought a sawmill in New Hope and in 1847 he purchased the property and replaced the sawmill with a grist and flour mill. He continued to build. He later constructed a distillery, a new sawmill and a large woollen mill, all in New Hope. It was largely his influence that brought the Great Western Railway to town in the 1850's, as an extension from Galt through Preston and New Hope to Guelph. In 1858, the village was incorporated and adopted the name Hespeler in recognition of Jacob Hespeler's tremendous contribution to the growth of the settlement.

One of the earliest steam-driven generating plants in Ontario lighted the homes and main streets in Hespeler. Owned by Joseph Shantz, this plant was operated in connection with a chopping mill west of the village. The municipality purchased this generating plant from Mr. Shantz in 1900. It is believed that this was the first instance of municipal ownership in Ontario.

The growth of the town continued steadily for the first half of the 20th century. Hespeler's industries in the 1950's included flour mills, a large woollen mill, stone works, and manufacturers of enamelware and steel tools. Prior to the amalgamation as part of Cambridge, Hespeler had a population of about 6,300.

The community of Blair, situated 3 miles northwest of Cambridge.

The third root of Cambridge is Galt. Galt began in 1816, when William Dickson, a Scottish merchant and member of the legislative council of Niagara, bought 92,000 acres of land on the present site of Galt. Dickson commissioned Absalom Shade, a carpenter from Pennsylvania, to build a settlement at the site. Shade set about building a two-storey log structure, opened a store and set up his headquarters. He then proceeded to erect a sawmill and grist mill in 1818. By 1820, the settlement appeared as a centre of activity with numerous buildings, including a distillery and a blacksmith shop. A road was opened between this hamlet and Guelph in 1827. The same year a post office opened and the settlement was named Galt in honour of John Galt, a Scottish novelist and William Dickson's close friend.

By the 1830's, a number of Scottish immigrants had settled in Galt and a flavour of heartiness and good cheer was prevalent. In 1834, the pioneers of Galt were exposed to a cholera epidemic. The disease had been introduced to the village by a company of travelling entertainers. Dr. Robert Miller, local physician and hero, travelled by horseback from home to home to administer to the community.

In 1850, Galt was incorporated as a village. Six years later, the Great Western Railway came to Galt. The resulting growth for the village produced industries that included two foundries, two flouring mills, a woollen mill, an axe factory, a distillery, a furniture factory, a brewery, a carriage factory, and a planing shop.

Galt was incorporated as a town in 1857, and a town hall erected in 1858. By 1915, the town was incorporated as a city. It continued to fourish as new and varied industries were established over the next several decades.

Cambridge, which is a part of the Regional Municipality of Waterloo, covers an area of over forty square miles. At the time of its formation the city had a population of 65,000 and within its boundaries were located 230 industries of every description.

Cambridge manufactures such diverse products as textiles, major household appliances, agricultural chemicals, plumbing and air conditioning equipment and nuclear and thermo steam-generating equipment.

These three roots have come together and leafed out into one strong and colourful city.

CHATHAM

William and Clara Stewart's wedding in Chatham, c. 1890's.

In 1794, Governor Simcoe chose the junction of the Thames River and McGregor's Creek as a strategic point for a naval shipyard for the defence of Upper Canada's western frontier. Simcoe feared that the tension between the United States and Britain might involve Upper Canada. He knew full well that Detroit might have to be ceded to the Americans and he hoped that building a fort in this new location would divert the Indian trade from Detroit. The Governor invited United Empire Loyalists, discharged soldiers, and any others to settle in the area. He also sent word to William Baker in Detroit, to ask him to supervise the construction of the naval establishment. Simcoe knew that Baker had been in charge of the Brooklyn navy yard under the British during the Revolutionary War. As an inducement to Baker to obtain his services as supervisor, Simcoe offered him several hundred acres of land along the Thames River and he chose to call it Chatham after Chatham, England along the Thames.

By the fall of 1794, William Baker and a crew of twenty-three men began the building of a blockhouse, a storehouse, and a number of gun boats. It was soon evident that the cost of maintaining a naval station exceeded Simcoe's earlier forecast. This fact, compounded by the selection of York as the Provincial seat of government instead of this new settlement, prompted Simcoe to abandon the new naval post. William Baker, now out of work, returned to Detroit after passing his land on to Joseph Eberts. Sergeant Mulhooland of the Queen's Rangers received orders to take charge of the abandoned site.

In 1795, Abraham Iredell was sent to the post to survey a town site of 600 acres surrounding the dockyards. In a very short time, thirty of the original 113 lots were settled. Iredell himself remained and built a log cabin and planted the first apple orchard in Kent County. By 1798, the blockhouse was removed to the town of Sandwich, under the supervision of Peter Russell, to be used as a courthouse and jail.

During the War of 1812, Tecumseh, the great Shawnee Chief, emerged as a famous ally of the British and fought numerous battles against the Americans. It was during one of these battles, under the command of General Proctor, that they were forced to retreat in the face of strong American forces. Tecumseh urged Proctor to halt at Chatham and make a stand. The General, disorganized and confused, continued his retreat upriver and left Tecumseh and his warriors to face the enemy alone near a swamp now called Moraviatown. Tecumseh was killed in the first skirmish. His son and the remainder of his force fled and returned later for the body of their beloved Chief. His body was never found. This military folly, and the subsequent death of Tecumseh, resulted in the courtmartial of General Proctor at Montreal in December of 1814 where he was sentenced to be publicly reprimanded.

In 1820, William Chrysler and his son, Henry, settled by the river and cleared some land. Henry built a blacksmith shop three years later on Third Street. Stephen Brook opened the first store in 1831.

In 1793, Parliament abolished slavery in Upper Canada, the first enactment of its kind in the British Empire. Fugitive slaves began to escape the bonds of slavery in the United States about 1800, and they crossed into Upper Canada seeking refuge. Their journey to freedom was assisted by the efforts of a network of people who transported slaves by railroad, by boat and by stagecoach – the Underground Railroad. By 1828, there were three negro families settled on the banks of McGregor's Creek. A year later they were joined by others, among them John Douglas, Charles Bakewell, James Stump and George Straws.

Chatham's growth increased in 1828, when a stagecoach route opened to Niagara and Detroit. A distillery and a steam sawmill were opened by Duncan McGregor in the 1830's. A bank opened in 1836 along with several stores and taverns. A crude bridge stretched across the

Men and mules building the railway near Chatham.

Thames River to welcome newcomers. In 1855 Chatham was incorporated as a town and by 1860 it had become the principal shipping port for products from the Thames River area.

Quite a stir occurred in Chatham in August, 1857, when two slave agents, John W. Wells of Lynchburg, Virginia, and T.G. James of Nashville, Tennessee, arrived in town to retrieve a fugitive slave. Word quickly circulated among the town blacks that they were looking for twenty-year-old Joseph Alexander. In a jiffy, a large crowd, including Joseph, assembled in front of the Royal Exchange Hotel where the men were staying. Mr. James addressed the crowd. He claimed that he had whipped Joseph only once, for drunkenness and the subsequent damage to his horse and carriage.

Joseph responded. James and Wells, he said, owned one of the largest slave pens in the South. Located behind the St. Charles Hotel in New Orleans, this pen held at least 500 slaves a day. When the Americans saw that the crowd could not be swayed, they offered Joseph a hundred dollars to accompany them to Windsor. This was his reply, "I am positive from what I know of James that as soon as he got me out he would shoot me dead and then leave me, for he would just as soon shoot a man as a black squirrel." The crowd promptly escorted the slavers to the train; Joseph Alexander had truly won his freedom that day.

One year later, John Brown, the ardent white abolitionist from Kansas arrived in Canada on April 29, 1858. He planned to overthrow the American government and with it the slave system. He selected Chatham as the ideal place to develop his military strategy, and draw up a constitution for a provisional government. He drilled his troops in Chatham's Tecumseh Park.

On October 16, 1859, John Brown and twenty-one followers attacked an American arsenal at Harpers Ferry, West Virginia. Of the twenty-one men who fought with Brown that day, ten were killed, six escaped, and five were later hanged. One Canadian, Stewart Taylor of Uxbridge, Ontario, died of wounds received in the raid. On December 2, 1859, John Brown was hanged in Charlestown, West Virginia. Two years later Americans and Canadians fought in a deadly civil war against slavery. Anderson Ruffin Abbott was the first Canadian-born black doctor who settled in Chatham in 1871 and set up practice there. There are a large number of black residents in Chatham today.

On April 17, 1895, the residents of Chatham celebrated in the streets when their town became a city.

The Chatham-Kent Museum facing Tecumseh Park was founded in 1943. Today it houses an excellent bird collection and native peoples' and pioneer artifacts including Tecumseh's warclub and powder horn, a rebel cannon captured in 1837, and a steam fire engine. The population today exceeds 38,000 and the churches number 32; there are two major hospitals and three college campuses as well as a number of international service clubs and organizations. The Chatham news was established in 1862 and is still the city's daily paper.

The city of Chatham remains prosperous, and proud of its early heritage; the sound of cannon fire and marching feet can be heard no longer on the grounds of Tecumseh Park; the past, evident only in the museum, remains largely hidden, the spirit of the land is free and very much Canadian.

CHATSWORTH

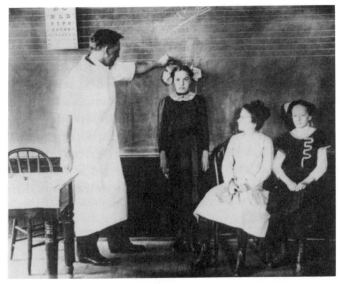

The doctor pays a visit to the school in Chatsworth.

Standing in the centre of a mixed farming area is the village of Chatsworth. Now some people might enquire as to the whereabouts of Chatsworth, or comment about never having heard of it. Chatsworth, to some, may seem like a tiny speck on the map of Ontario, but to those folks residing within the village limits, Chatsworth is worthy of mention. The memory of those who first arrived here and cleared the timber to make way for others to live in a harmonious setting is quite noteworthy. They created a place where one could feel they belonged, and for some, a place that provided opportunity to own land and raise a family in peace.

On the Garafraxa Colonization road, along the western boundary of Holland Township, a Mr. Coyer stopped on his journey and built a log tavern. This was on the south side of the present village. If he had continued another eight miles north, he would have reached Owen Sound. The building was replaced later by a frame structure and called "The Caribou House" and later still the Campbell House.

The land on which most of Chatsworth stands was once owned by George and John Deavitt. For this reason, the early settlement was first named Johntown.

As the village grew, a post office was needed and a postmaster by the name of Henry Cardwell made that provision. It is conjectured that Cardwell suggested the name of Chatsworth for the village after his home in England.

In 1873, the Toronto, Grey and Bruce Railway reached Chatsworth. The village quickly developed, and was supported by shipping grain. By the late 1880's, Chatsworth had quite a pretentious hotel that was called the California House and became well known for its entertainment. Twelve stores lined the streets, a large foundry, several wagon and blacksmith shops, a sawmill, a shingle mill, one school and four churches. The village at one time even had two rival newspapers.

Chatsworth may not be as large as it once was, but one piece of history that has remained and that still prospers is the Agricultural Fair. The fair has been in or near the village every year since 1860. Agricultural products such as natural honey are available to travellers through this community.

✦

CLINTON

The town of Clinton is located at the junction of what were once known as the Huron and London Roads, and are now Highway 8 and 4, respectively. Clinton is one of the few small towns in Ontario that has had nine different newspapers, from The Courier to The News Record, which is still being published today.

The earliest settlers to arrive were Jonas Givving and Stephen Vanderburg in 1831. Vanderburg built a log tavern that was eventually operated by William Rattenbury in 1844.

It was Rattenbury who was considered the founder of Clinton. Originally a blacksmith, he bought land in the village in 1855, and laid out lots for settlement. He called the community Clinton in honour of Lord Clinton, on whose land in England his father was a tenant farmer.

One early settler, by the name of Joseph Whitehead, was a mechanical engineer and played an indirect role in bringing Clinton many steam-powered industries. He later became the first reeve of Clinton when it

The main street of Clinton before the turn of the century.

became incorporated as a village in 1857.

In 1875, when Clinton became a town, large deposits of salt were found in the area and the McGarva Works and the Stapleton Salt Works were established. By that time the town had two sawmills operating, a steam bending factory, three planing mills, a sash, door and blind factory, a carding mill, a flax mill and an organ factory. For accommodation and entertainment the town at one point had five hotels and a saloon.

One of Clinton's most colourful citizens, who contributed to the development of the town, was Horatio Hale. He was an American lawyer who arrived in Clinton to evaluate land holdings on behalf of his wife's family, the Pughs. He liked the place so much and was so drawn to studying the native Mohawk culture, that he stayed. He is now recognized as one of North America's pioneer ethnologists and linguists. It was through his efforts that the first library was built.

Clinton is located on the CNR line and is only thirteen miles southeast of Goderich, which is a considerable port. These two factors have contributed to the development of Clinton as a distributing centre. A number of industries make up its employment force and unique among these is a piano factory. Today it has a population of more than 3,000 people.

COLLINGWOOD

Fishing fleet in the Collingwood Harbour, c. 1885.

Collingwood was originally known as Hen-and-Chickens Harbour, an apt description of the one large and four small off-shore islands, that have since become part of the mainland. The mainland was covered with dense bush, tangled tamaracks and cedar swamp. The locality seemed so uninviting that there was no thought of developing a town at Hen-and-Chickens Harbour until the railway engineers chose it to be the northern terminus of the Ontario, Simcoe, and Huron Railway. This line linked Toronto on Lake Ontario to the waters of Lake Huron. The railway was renamed the Northern Railway of Canada in 1858.

The small community of Hurontario Mills on the shore of Pretty River, began in 1840. This settlement, once separate and one mile to the east, is now part of Collingwood and is known locally as the old village.

The first settler to arrive in the area was George Carney in 1835 and he was followed by Joel Underwood, an American, in 1847. In 1852 Underwood purchased 335 acres of land, across from the hen and her chicks. He supplied the land to erect a steam sawmill, a business that became the economic nucleus for the future city.

Collingwood was chosen to be the name of this place. It had been the name of a township in Simcoe County. The township, in turn, had been named in honour of the English admiral, Lord Cuthbert Collingwood.

In 1853, the population consisted of several families, William Watt, a fisherman and his crew; Underwood, a sawmiller; Loomis, a railway construction agent; Cosgrove, a boardinghouse keeper; and George Collins, a tavernkeeper.

Work progressed on a pier and a breakwater in the harbour. The arrival of railway construction workers helped to attract population to the settlement. The railway was completed in 1855, and that same year the first line of steamers sailed between Collingwood, Ontario and Erie, Pennsylvania. Collingwood became a busy trans-shipping point for grain from the mid-western United States. It arrived by barge and was then forwarded by rail to Toronto. Lumber rafts from the northern forest often filled the harbour, en route to the south.

The settlement grew so quickly that it was incorporated as a town in 1858, without ever having been incorporated as a village. The activities of the town reflected the hurried pace of development. Hector McAllister built Collingwood's first boat and Andrew Lockerbee started machine shops for the repair of vessels. Numerous mills and hotels sprang up around town. In 1870, the largest grain elevator on the Great Lakes was built at Collingwood. In 1882, Collingwood issued debentures to the amount of $25,000 to assist in building and establishing a Dry Dock and a Shipbuilding Yard in town. Other industries included the Wilson Manufacturing Company, the Imperial Steel and Wire plant, the Telfar Biscuit Company, a canning factory, the Georgian Bay Fish Company, the Northern Navigation Company, and the Charlton Lumber Company.

Several fires have occurred in the town at different times, but the one on Sunday, September 25, 1881, was the most disastrous of them all. The fire swept through a large portion of Hurontario Street (the main throughfare) in the business section of the town.

Steamships figured prominently in the life of Collingwood and other Great Lake ports. Majestic and increasingly palatial vessels like the luxurious J.B. Maxwell, a paddlewheeler with tall stacks, wood panelled staterooms and grand dining salon, made runs from Midland and Penetanguishene to Parry Sound. The City of Midland, which sailed out of Collingwood; and much later the City of Parry Sound, City of Collingwood, Majestic City of Toronto and several others were the luxury liners of the inland sea. They were capable of accommodating up to 1,000 passengers in style and in comfort.

Those were the days when very few cottages dotted the Georgian Bay shoreline. It was only a matter of time before the more well-to-do families from Buffalo, Detroit, Rochester, New York, Cleveland and Toronto discovered the sandy beaches and shadowed bays of points farther north. These vacationers erected lavish and gracious two-storey buildings with wide verandahs. These summer cottages were garnished with ornate gingerbread and stained glass windows. Others arrived with houseboats that had been built on large scows and were towed by steam tugs to sheltered bays. They dropped anchor here from early July until Labour Day weekend. This marked the end of the tranquil waters and isolated communities and was the birth of a new industry, tourism.

In 1946, a Czechoslovakian refugee by the name of Jozo Weider appeared in Collingwood. This native of mountainous central Europe turned his attention to Blue Mountain. In a short time he built a ski area that now covers 1,000 acres. His second love in life was pottery and with skiing underway, he devoted his energies to this industry. Collingwood became the "Pottery Capital of Canada" with six factories turning out products that are internationally known and popular – Blue Mountain Pottery.

The heart of Collingwood has always been shipbuilding. Over the years many great ships have been built here in the Collingwood yards. The great bulk-carrier Agawa, launched in 1902 and Canada Steam Ship Lines giant Simcoe measuring 750 feet in length, sporting three 12,000-pound anchors, and capable of carring a million bushels of grain were both built in Collingwood.

The ice man – William Swain – on his rounds in Collingwood, around 1875.

In December, 1939, the newly-formed Canadian War Supply Board asked for tenders for the building of corvettes and minesweepers in Canada. Two months later contracts were approved with twelve Canadian Companies, including Collingwood Shipyards Limited. The board authorized the building of three Flower-class corvettes in 1940 and another five the following year. The price was set at $528,000 per vessel and as a result there was increased employment and economic prosperity for Collingwood. More than two hundred steel ships have sailed out of the Collingwood Bay Shipyards to various watery destinies.

Although the shipbuilding boom tapered off in later years it is still in operation. Collingwood's agricultural economy has continued strong. The Collingwood area has always been the fruit grower of Simcoe County and apples are the primary crop.

The winds blow from a different direction in Collingwood today. Gone are the days of the steamer. The harbour is somewhat quieter and the mountain in the distance is somewhat busier. People have become a major industry of Collingwood. The hurried pace of bodies in motion have supplanted the softer rhythms and the deliberate trot of horses.

COOKSTOWN

The village site where Cookstown sits today was first surveyed in 1820. Between 1825-1830, a large number of Irish immigrants put down roots here. The settlement was situated at the corners of four townships, Innisfill, Essa, Tecumseh, and West Gwillimbury. John Perry arrived in the autumn of 1826 and erected a tavern on the northeast corner of the village. Mr Dixon settled in and built a tavern on the Essa corner, known as Dixon's Corners. Thomas Cook of Caven, Ireland, came in 1831; he divided his land grant into lots and the site became Cook's Town.

In 1867, the Cookstown town hall was built on Hamilton Street as a Temperance Hall, by the Independent Order of Good Templers. They felt the hall was needed to offset the effects of four hotels, a liquor store and several grocery stores – all selling pure whiskey at cheap prices. They kept the Hall active for over fifty years with entertainment and activities. The building is now used as a theatre and concert hall.

The H. Couse General and Feed Store in Cookstown, c. 1904.

Cookstown at the end of the 1920's was a complete community. A walk along Queen Street and King Street would take you past a bakery, a shoe store, a drug store, a furniture store, a funeral parlour, two hotels, three barber shops, a newspaper office, a grocery store, a meat market, three general stores, two hardware stores, a shoe repair shop, a Chinese laundry, two garages, two dry goods outlets, a dentist's office, two doctors' offices, a lumber yard and mill, a bank, a telephone office, an insurance broker's, the post office, the United Church and the village jail.

The business section along the Canadian National Railway tracks that crossed Queen Street included stock yards, a flour mill, a creamery, grain elevators, feed storage bins, a cheese factory, an evaporator, two blacksmiths and a harness-making shop.

By 1974, the scene had changed. Gone were most of the farm-related industries. Only the unused flour mill was still standing. The newspaper, the hotels, the cheese factory, the Chinese laundry, the meat market, the dentist, and the telephone office were all gone. Many of the buildings on the main street were empty; others were torn down.

Cookstown had transformed from an economically self-sufficient community to one almost completely dependent on other centres. The last passenger train to stop at Cookstown travelled through on July 2,

1960. By 1967, the Canadian National Railway station had closed down. As the older residents passed away, their stately homes were purchased by Toronto commuters. The young people of the village had left to seek a higher education and professional and business futures that could no longer be found at home. By 1973 more town residents worked in Toronto, Barrie and Camp Borden than were employed within the village.

In the last few years Cookstown has become a favourite haunt of antique craft hunters. Every other shop sells collectibles. The rich Victorian-influenced 19th-century architecture exists on both sides of the main street. The stores are decorated with gingerbread trim, pointed Gothic gables, decorative brickwork and verandahs. The district is dotted with L-shaped farmhouses. Cookstown has managed to return again to its former splendour through the tourist trade instead of disappearing as a ghost town.

DRESDEN

In 1825, Jared Lindsley settled on the present site of Dresden and sold his property to the Van Allen family of Chatham in the 1840's. It was Daniel Van Allen who laid out a town plot in 1852, between the Sydenham River and what later became main street.

Prior to the 1840's a number of fugitive slaves from the United States had arrived in Camden Township in the Dresden area. The Reverend Josiah Henson, a former slave who had escaped in 1830 to Upper Canada, purchased, with the help of abolitionists, 200 acres of land in the Dresden district in 1841. Henson soon established a vocational school for fugitive slaves, called the British American Institute. To provide employment for his students, he erected a sawmill and a grist mill on his property; to continue the services he provided for his people, the reverend travelled far and wide on lecture tours to raise the necessary funds to operate his centre. Meanwhile, the institute was left in the hands of an incompetent manager and the workers left in search of better wages. The end result was that the Institute was torn down and the property sold. Part of the money received from the sale of the land went to the construction of the Wilberforce Institute. This establishment was in turn torn down when a new high school was built.

The immortalized "Uncle Tom" of Harriet Beecher Stowes' famous novel, Reverend Henson was buried near his home. This house, along with six museum buildings and two graveyards, highlights the earlier historical passage of Dresden.

In 1852, William Wright, who was a hotel keeper and who owned the land adjacent to the Van Allens, surveyed his property into lots and called the settlement Fairport. The name Dresden was chosen by postal authorities when a post office opened in 1854. Some people believe the name was chosen in honour of the city of Dresden in eastern Germany.

Dresden's early prosperity centered around timber resources and the navigation facilities provided by the Sydenham River and resulted in the settlement expanding to the north shore of the river. Dresden, with a population of 750, incorporated as a village in 1871 and a town hall was erected in 1875. By 1881, the population had reached 2,000 and Dresden became a town.

The present-day population sits at about 2,500 people and some of the economic base has changed but the basic flavour was established a long time ago. Industry today focuses on wheels, spokes, hubs, canned goods, flour, cement blocks and die-cast products; agricultural growers concentrate on wheat, sugar beets, corn and tomatoes.

Over the course of the years Dresden has kept abreast with the times. The population has grown but not to city size and it remains one of the more unique small towns of Ontario. Nevertheless, few towns have played such a vital role in addressing and encouraging the freedom of all peoples. Uncle Tom's Cabin stands here as a wonderful reminder to us all.

DUNDAS

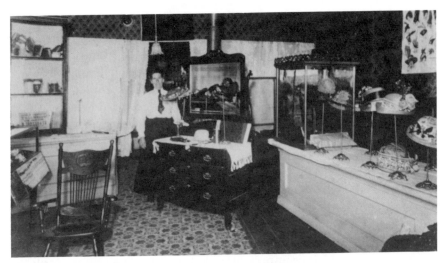

The interior of a millinery shop in Dundas, c. 1914.

In 1787, Anne Morden walked cautiously inland from Hamilton through the wilderness valley accompanied only by her sons and daughters. A loyalist widow, without the company of a grown man, she continued determined. She was undaunted by the knowledge that the year before seven hundred mississauga rattlesnakes were killed by pioneers near Burlington Bay. When she finally reached land she put down roots on a site comprising the northern half of the Town of Dundas.

Two years later, the Shower family arrived and settled opposite of the Mordens. Soon other settlers came, and this small settlement came to be known as Coote's Paradise, after a Captain Thomas Coote. The captain often came to hunt in the adjacent swamp, which teemed with waterfowl. Mrs. John Graves Simcoe, in her diary, describes Coote's Paradise as "a place that abounds with wildfowl and tortoises; from hence it appears more like a river or lake than a marsh".

To promote settlement in the western part of Upper Canada, Lieutenant Governor Simcoe, in 1793, ordered a military road to be built between Lake Ontario and the River Thames. The road was named in honour of the Honourable Henry Dundas, British Secretary of State for War and Colonies. At the eastern terminus of the road, Simcoe authorized a town plot where Mrs. Morden had settled.

Mills were erected and by 1808, streets were laid out. By 1819, there were two taverns and three storehouses in the settlement. A distillery and hotel operated by Manuel Overfield once stood on the site of the town hall. Edward Peer was also busy building a road to Hamilton known as Peer's Road.

In 1823, the government authorized the construction of a canal to facilitate movement of large vessels through the Burlington sandbar. Such a canal would have rendered the shallow approach through Coote's Paradise marsh at Dundas. He did not live to see it completed in 1837 but, thanks to his foresight, Dundas began to develop and, for a time, became the most important town west of Toronto, surpassing even St. Catharines and Hamilton. Unfortunately, when the Great Western Railway was built in 1853, the Desjardins Canal quickly diminished in significance.

In 1847, the village of Dundas and the community of Dundas Mills were incorporated as a town. Two years later, in July of 1849, the town hall of Dundas was completed. The stone building design was a version of Roman Classic by Francis Hawkins of Dundas, and the construction was by James Scott. This impressive structure is among Ontario's oldest surviving municipal buildings.

By the mid-1800's Dundas had a good variety of industries; a large woollen and cotton mill were in operation along with agricultural implement factories and a basketmaking company.

Dundas has always remained attractive to those wishing to settle down and take root. Today the town has become a large residential centre for those who work in nearby Hamilton, and it still remains a retail distribution point as well as an industrial centre. Dundas is certainly worth a visit to admire the outstanding collection of costumes, china and glass and a selection of antique toys and dolls at the Dundas Historical Society Museum located at the corner of Park and Albert Streets. Manufacturing still goes on and products range from office and church furniture to machinery for mining, communications, and electronics to clothing, gloves and knitwear. Tourists and Sunday recreation seekers come to enjoy the wonderful varieties of ice cream at the Dundas dairy, to walk the Bruce Trail which looks out over the lake and to stand beneath the falls or romp in the park at Webster's Falls Conservation area.

Anne Morden was a brave woman who certainly demonstrated the equality between men and women. She and Mary Gage of Stoney Creek had nothing to prove nor any statements to make; they simply worked to survive.

DUNNVILLE

A view of Canal Street in Dunnville during the flood of 1913.

Solomon Minor was the first to settle on the site of the present town of Dunnville in 1825. The site was on the scenic Grand River just four miles north of Lake Erie. There he constructed a dam across the river to harness the necessary water power to operate mills.

Oliver Phelps arrived shortly after Minor and purchased three lots in the vicinity and had them laid out into a village plot. Settlers soon came and erected the necessary buildings to house their families. The settlement is believed to have been named for the Honourable Henry Dunn, Receiver General of Upper Canada at that time.

In 1829, The Welland Canal Company, founded by William Hamilton Merritt of St. Catharines, selected Dunnville as the terminus of a feeder canal to the Welland Canal. The Canada Company offered perpetual exemption from water rent to the first manufacturing enterprise to be operating after the feeder canal was completed. The Company hoped that this would encourage some industrial growth for the area.

The race was on! Oliver Phelps of Dunnville jumped at the opportunity; Mr. Keffer at Thorold did too. Keefer's mill was the first to be completed but Phelps cut corners by having his machinery installed before the roof was put on. As a result, Phelps was able to grind the first bushel of wheat as soon as the water was let into the canal and before it had a chance to reach Keffer's mill. In an attitude of fairness, the company awarded the free water privileges to both of these industrious entrepreneurs.

In 1854, the residents of Dunnville met in a schoolhouse and formed a Library Association. One hundred and thirty citizens paid one pound each towards the purchase of a library and a stock of 660 books.

Dunnville was incorporated as a village in 1860 and as a town by 1900. By the 1970's the manufacturing industries included ladies' suits, sweaters, hosiery, towels, drapes, fish nets, guns, chemicals, and canned goods. The town newspaper is The Chronicle which has been in publication since 1896.

Tourism, today, plays a vital role in Dunnville's economy. Numerous tourists arrive to camp and swim at Rock Point Provincial Park situated eleven kilometers southeast of Dunnville. Quality leisure time can be spent viewing the bird life and the unusual flora and searching for fossils in the park. The Grand River is as grand and scenic today as it was in yesteryear.

DURHAM

In the spring of 1842, Archibald Hunter, a Scotsman, led a group of settlers northward over the Garafraxa colonization road. He had been assured by surveyors that there was excellent farm land north of the Saugeen River.

At the Saugeen, they located a crossing where the course of the river could provide ample current to power a mill, and decided to settle there. Their location was just twenty-eight miles southeast of Owen Sound.

That summer Archibald built a log house to reside in for the winter. The next spring he journeyed to New York State where his family was waiting to accompany him to their new home.

As more settlers began to move northward past Archibald Hunter's door to locate on the free grants of land, he opened that door to the public. This proved to be advantageous for settlers and prospectors, since there was no inn between Mount Forest and Owen Sound. In 1854, he constructed a large stone building known as the British Hotel.

Bentinck was the first name of the settlement after the township, and later it was changed to Durham by Crown Lands Agent, George Jackson of Durham, England.

In 1851, the Durham Road, another important settlement road, reached Durham and crossed the Owen Sound Road. This helped to accelerate the growth of the hamlet.

An Irishman named John Edge arrived in 1847, and built a flour mill, followed by a sawmill and a woollen mill. The flour mill operated on a large export trade. The processed wheat was transported by team to Guelph and then by rail to points distant.

In 1850, Owen Sound was appointed county town instead of Durham. The community of Durham suffered a temporary setback, but by the 1870's the village had a considerable number of industries.

Without ever having been incorporated as a village, Durham became a town in 1872, when the Townships of Bentinck and Glenelg were separated. Three years later the town hall was built on Garafraxa Street, and later moved to its present site.

The two major industries in Durham both came into being at the turn of the century. The first was the Durham Furniture Company Limited, founded in 1899 with Dr. David Jamieson as president. The plant was totally rebuilt in 1905 after fire completely destroyed it. Nevertheless the industry continued to grow and thrive and became part of the well-known Krochler Manufacturing Company. Durham is renowned for its fine furniture and annually hosts a major wood show. The Canadian Collectibles show is also held here each August.

The National Portland Cement Company started business in 1901 and prospered in Durham for several years. It was taken over by the Consolidated Sand and Gravel Company and later by the Durham Crushed Stone Company.

Industry and agriculture have combined to make Durham a viable community. One hundred and fifty years later this town endures and thrives. The beautiful Saugeen still flows with the same current that made it a choice location in the first place.

ELMIRA

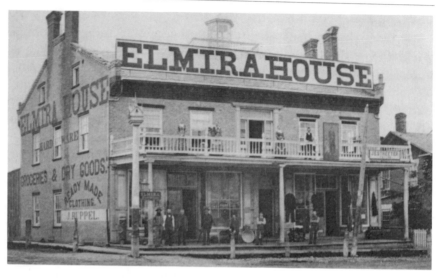

The Elmira House and Post Office, built in 1860.

Any visitor to Elmira will be astonished to see, in this age of the automobile, the number of horse-drawn vehicles that line the streets. Many of the local people of Elmira cling to the old, simple way of life, and shun the technological advances that came with modern industrialization. These people call themselves Mennonites. For them a clock to measure the day and year does not exist. They live by the sun and the changing seasons of the land. They are a proud race of people.

Elmira got its start when Edward Bristow came here to establish a lodging in the 1830's. Soon others joined him; George Streetor, Thomas Walker, James Gass, and Robert Canning purchased lots nearby.

Edward Bristow opened a tavern in 1843 and was also the first to open a store in the hamlet. The settlement became known as Bristow's Corners. When a post office was established in Bristow's store in 1853 the name changed to West Woolich. In 1867, the community received the name Elmira.

Messrs. Good and Winger were responsible for laying out the village streets and lots. Craftsmen were drawn to the new settlement and among the first of these were Henry and Hiram Martin who established a furniture company.

In 1886, Elmira with a population of 800, became an incorporated village. The early residents were of British extraction, but by the end of the 19th century, many German and Pennsylvania Dutch settlers had arrived. A German language paper entitled *The Signet* first appeared in the village in 1893.

Most of the farms in the district are operated by old-order Mennonites who come to town to sell their wares and purchase necessary supplies. The community is an interesting blend of the old and of the new, in atmosphere and commerce. Every spring the Mennonite maple-syrup festival attracts visitors from as far away as the United States.

Although farming is the mainstay of Elmira's economy, manufacturing has an important role. The range of products includes furniture, chemicals, fertilizers, clothing, butter, wood and aluminum specialities.

There are supply stores that are set up the way stores once were – bulk products in bins and weigh scales and paper bags; there are craft stores that specialize in Mennonite handiwork such as quilts, wooden children's toys and foodstuffs. These businesses may seem to others to be quaint but to the Mennonite people they are an expression of the way things should really be everywhere – efficient, practical and wholesome.

Set in the rich farmlands of the Grand and Conestoga River valleys, Elmira is a focal point for all people to study their early roots and focus on their feelings about life without the automobile, electricity or gas. Here the visitor can observe the farms and people living the way that all people once did in this country. It is truly an amazing opportunity to see a style of life that for most people will only be found in books.

ELORA

Perched in the middle of the falls stands a reminder of the powers of nature. Like a torch, the tooth of time, long known as the Islet Rock, it heralds the beginning of four miles of a water-carved, limestone ravine. It was to this spot that the Neutral Indians fled to hide their precious wampum beads after the great battle of 1651 between the Hurons and the Iroquois at the present-day site of Hamilton. Those were the times when

An early street scene from Elora.

inland villages were abandoned and the Iroqois swept unresisted over the whole peninsula. In those dark days many Neutral Indians availed themselves of the shelter of the ravines and caves of the Elora Gorge. So powerful and lasting is the image of the Rock, it is now the symbol of the village of Elora.

The first white settler to come to Elora, the town at the junction of the Grand and Irvine Rivers, fifteen miles northwest of Guelph, was Roswell Mathews. A Welshman from the United States, he arrived here in 1817. As a carpenter and millwright, he was contracted to build a dam and sawmill for James Crooks who was the agent for General Pilkington. The site chosen was down the river by the cascade. Unfortunately, he was unable to secure a solid footing and the dam washed away in the spring floods. With a surplus of wheat and nowhere to mill it, marketing became a problem, a problem left to him to solve. He and his sons hollowed out a pine log thirty feet long. He launched his dugout a mile and a half below the falls, loaded it with sixteen bags of wheat, and paddled down to Galt where he sold his wheat for fifty cents a bushel. The dugout was sold for $2.50. They returned on foot.

Following a number of disappointing years watching his work swept away by the Grand River in the spring floods, he left the area.

Elora languished then until the arrival of Captain Gilkinson in 1832.

Gilkinson, a cousin of John Galt, founder of the city of Guelph, was a native of Irvine, Scotland. He planned a new settlement at the junction of the Grand and Irvine Rivers, near a falls. Recently retired from Lake service with the Northwest Fur Trading Company, the captain purchased 14,000 acres of land at a reported $2.50 an acre. He named his new village Elora to reflect the similarity of caves near the falls to the famous Elora Temple of India.

Before his untimely death the next year, Gilkinson had established a sawmill and a general store in Elora. Soon the hamlet boasted a tavern, a blacksmith shop and a post office which was opened in 1839. In the 1840's James Ross and Company purchased the two acres around the falls and commissioned a local carpenter named Charles Allan to build a wood-frame mill. Prior to this many people walked long distances carrying a bag of flour or provisions from Dundas, Hamilton and Galt. With the mill in operation the village grew dramatically, reaching a population of 1200 by the late 1850's.

The other factor contributing to growth was road improvement. For years the country between Elora and Huron was mostly uninterrupted bush with only a few patches where clearings were made. A story is told about a mother in Scotland who had written to her son somewhere in the area commonly known as the Queen's Bush. The only address on the letter was, "To my son John in the bush." He received the letter.

Ankle-deep in the Elora Gorge.

The village of Elora was centered on the south side of a large square area which, it is said, was planned for the town hall site. The square was approached from the west by Woolwich Street, from the east by McNab Street and by a wide street from the Grand River in the north, known as Gilkinson Street.

The first Methodist church was a log building built in 1844. A Catholic Church, constructed around the same time, stood near the old red brick school on the Elora Guelph Road. An Anglican Church, completed in 1842, occupied a site at the extreme western end of Woolwich, just over the townline in Pilkington Township. Only the old graveyard indicated where the church stood. The church is said to have been a replica of the old church on the Indian Reserve at Brantford.

The house of Mr. Thomas McManus on Walnut Street was known as Martin's Tavern. The oldest house, still standing, was the first Post Office near the water tower and south of the river. Early stories say that the tavern was haunted, stories arising no doubt from tales of a murder committed there.

The first business street was Victoria Street, with three new stores in 1852, but it was along Mill and Lower Metcalfe Streets that the first real business centre developed in the 1860's. Among the stores doing business in this section were Adam Fries, tailor; Mrs. Sinclair, general store; Miss Eliza Massie, milliner; Wm. Knowles, hardware; the Penetentiary shoe store operated by Wm. Kerr.

At the south end of Victoria bridge there was a plant which manufactured a shredded wood product known as "Escelsiot". The termination of this concern was somewhat different from others of its contemporaries: it was not flooded out or burnt down – it blew up. At the quiet hour of noon, June 13, 1891, the village was shaken as if by an earthquake. The boiler of the Exelsior factory had exploded, completely demolishing the building in which it was housed and, unfortunately, killing the fireman, Mr. William Ariss.

From 1862 until well into the 1870's there was a building boom in which many public and private buildings were erected – Methodist Church 1862, Town Hall 1874, Drill shed (Armoury Hall) 1865, Dalby House 1865, St. Mary's Church 1870, Knox Church 1873, St. John's 1875, Chalmers Presbyterian (Pottery) 1876, Kirk and Clarke store 1861, Baptist Church 1863, Grammar School (stone) 1864, burned 1874.

In 1857 several Indians from the shores of the Upper Lakes visited Elora in search of the treasure which their forefathers had hidden among the rocks by the singing waters. The Indians soon left without discovering anything. Little did they know that a few yards from a place the settlers called the hole-in-the-rock is a cave in the face of the cliff in the Elora Gorge. There in the cave the Neutral Indians two hundred years before had hidden their precious wampum beads. It wasn't until a Sunday afternoon in 1880, that two boys, Foxy Hillis and Corky MacDonald, found several of the wampum beads which had been washed from the cave by an unusually heavy rain. The boys told their teacher, David Boyle, and he carefully sifted the fine earth from the cave and secured the treasure which the Indians had failed to find. Some of those beads are in the Royal Ontario Museum in Toronto.

Today the village of Elora still appears as it did when it was incorporated in 1858. Gone are the horse and buggy days, but the early architecture of this settlement remains unchanged.

The Elora Gorge, which is part of a park, attracts many visitors each year. In the village there are numerous reminders of the pioneer days – old mills by the river and lovely old churches, such as St. John's Anglican. The communion set in this church is said to have been the gift of Florence Nightingale, heroine of the Crimean War and cousin to one of the pastors there.

Down by the falls on Mill Street stands the Elora Mill. These buildings are today very different from the past. Once the mill was surrounded by a variety of wooden sheds for storage of all manner of equipment but today, four outbuildings house many fine guest rooms and facilities for visitors. The entire street, much like all of downtown Elora, is lined with antique, craft and specialty shops. To see all there is to see in Elora can take an entire weekend. The Wellington County Musuem and Archives, located just outside of town is a day's outing if you include a picnic lunch and a cool swim in the stone quarry by the Grand River just down the road.

EXETER

The picturesque town of Exeter situated on the Ausable River was named for the town of Exeter in Devonshire, England.

James Willis and his family were the first to arrive here in 1832 via the London Colonization Road. That first winter their nearest neighbour lived twenty miles distant. The next spring saw the arrival of William McConnell who erected a shanty just a few miles from Willis's log home.

McConnell was employed as a contractor by the Canada Company to build the London Road through as far as Huron County. His payment for the work was land and in addition he purchased land on both sides of London Road. Here stands the town of Exeter.

That fall McConnell erected a sawmill on the Ausable River near to where it crossed the London Road. A year later he built a grist mill, and this settlement became Francistown.

South of Francistown, Isaac Carling built a store and tannery in 1847. Then came the arrival of James Pickard, an Englishman who opened a general store. A village plot was laid out here and soon the settlement of Exeter became the chief market centre of the area.

Several of the early pioneers had come from Devonshire, England and were loyal to the Methodist sect called the Bible Christian Society.

In the year 1873, village leaders petitioned the government to amalgamate and incorporate the locations of Exeter and Francistown as the village Exeter. Incorporation occurred on March 29, 1873.

The 1880's exemplified the sucess of the amalgamation. Business enterprises flourished. The village hosted numerous stores, six hotels, two chartered banks and a private bank. Industries included were mills - tannery, saw, flax, flour, grist and woollen.

The town experienced steady industrial growth in the 20th century. Although some earlier enterprises disappeared, new ones took their places. An extensive canning industry plays a major role in the economic base today and farms in the area concentrate on crops of wheat, peas, beans, corn and livestock. Lumber mills and furniture factories still flourish and house trailers and farm machinery are manufactured in the area.

Today the population is close to 3,400 and reveals a strong heritage of rich agricultural land.

FERGUS

Street scene of Fergus in 1895.

Few towns in Ontario the size of Fergus feature such splendid Scottish limestone architecture as is seen here. The outstanding characteristic of this town is the existence of some two hundred buildings constructed by Scottish stonemasons during the nineteenth century.

Situated on the banks of the Grand River, in the heart of Wellington County, the town was named after Adam Ferguson, a Scottish lawyer. Ferguson arrived in Canada in 1831 to explore colonization possibilities for the Highland Society of Scotland. His journey led him to Niagara Falls and then north to Guelph. Completely enthralled by the beauty of the countryside, he returned to Scotland and persuaded a fellow lawyer, by the name of James Webster, to emigrate with him to Canada.

Ferguson, accompanied by six of his seven sons, and Webster arrived at the banks of the Grand River in 1833, with deed and title to 7,300 acres of land. In short order, four streets were laid out and log houses were erected. Within a year Fergus boasted seventy inhabitants.

In 1834, Adam Ferguson constructed a primitive bridge across the Grand, and the following year Hugh Black opened a tavern in the village. For some unknown reason, Ferguson left to settle in Waterdown just northwest of Burlington. Two of his sons remained behind and likewise his friend James Webster.

It is noteworthy that all of the early pioneers of Fergus were well-educated and were of Scottish descent. Their first log school house was built in 1836 to maintain that standard of education. Before long these Scottish settlers were busy replacing their log homes with fine limestone houses, not unlike those in the old country.

In 1858, Fergus was incorporated as a village when its population had reached a thousand. The industrial sector of the hamlet by that time encompassed several sawmills, flax and woollen mills, distilleries, breweries, tanneries, foundries, and a stave factory. A sewing-machine factory was one of the busiest local industries during the 1870's. The Templin Carriage and Wagon Works, begun in 1869, manufactured sleighs and later became an automobile sales outlet.

The oldest curling club west of Kingston was founded in Fergus during the 1830's by Hugh Black. Fergus residents first took up the game of lacrosse in the 1860's. One of the oldest established fall fairs in Ontario is the Wellington County Fair, started in Fergus, in 1837.

The first doctor to perform an appendectomy in North America was a Fergus doctor by the name of Dr. Abraham Groves. He was also the man who opened a hospital in Fergus in the year 1902. Dr. Groves went on to found a training school for nurses and today the Groves Memorial Hospital honours his contributions.

The Scottish heritage in Fergus has continued strong, and is especially expressed during the Highland Games held annually in mid-August since 1946. The highland band and the brass band, in Fergus, never disappoint the crowds.

The hymn "The Ninety and Nine" was written in honour of a Fergus resident, George Clephane, who died in 1851. Fergus had another famous citizen in the person of Patrick Bell. His invention of the reaping machine revolutionized agricultural labour and the timing of harvests became less precarious.

Fergus has been a town since 1953 and today it has 6,000 residents. The Wellington County Museum is open all year and contains a variety of articles relating to Fergus and the county. The museum is located between Elora and Fergus.

FLESHERTON

The village of Flesherton showed great promise in becoming a town until the railway line arrived. It passed west of the hamlet by a mile and a half. This marked a significant decline in industry, population and growth.

Situated thirty miles southeast of Owen Sound, Flesherton owes its existence to W.K. Flesher, an English-born settler who purchased land at the crossroads in 1853. He built a dam on the fast-moving waters of the Boyne River, a tributary of the Beaver River, and erected a sawmill and a grist mill. It was here, on a portion of his property, that village lots were staked out.

Flesherton's first permanent resident was Aaron Munshaw, who settled here in 1849 and opened a tavern for stagecoach travellers. The tavern was situated across from the present-day cemetery. To the north of this he built another hotel in the 1860's. It still stands as an historic landmark in the village.

Flesher's Mills also attracted many other businesses to the area. At one time the business community of Flesherton hosted a woollen mill, a pump factory, four general stores, one drug store, two large cabinet factories, a tannery, a cheese factory, and a number of carriage, blacksmith, harness and tailor shops. Several hotels operated in town, including the Boyne Water Hotel which was located on the north bank of the Boyne River across from the present school.

The first post office in the township was established here in 1851. For the settlers this meant that they no longer had to travel thirty miles to Orangeville to post a letter.

During the early growth of the settlement people called their home Flesher's Corners. As the community expanded beyond the corners, the name Flesherton was adopted in honour of the founder. A dignified and enterprising man, Flesher established the first Masonic Lodge in the village, organized the militia, served as a member of parliament, and was both warden of the county and reeve of Artemesia Township.

The Flesherton Woollen mill was started in 1863 by Peter Campbell and sold to John Nuhn in 1894. His son, John Jr., inherited the mill in 1931 and four years later it burned down, to be replaced by a smaller one. During World War Two the Nuhns sold thousands of wool blankets to the

Red Cross in Toronto. In later years they made cheaper blankets by combining re-claimed wool with new wool. John Jr. died in 1954 and although his wife kept the business for some time it did eventually get sold.

A planing mill and wood-working shop manufactured window frames, sashes, doors, trim and mouldings. When livestock trucking came into being truck racks were added to this list of wood products. It was destoryed once by fire, rebuilt in 1953, and continued in operation until 1981. Today it is used for storage.

Flesherton remains as the crossroads of the township. Its foundations are lodged deeply in the memories of its early pioneers, and reflect a spirit of life as strong as the Boyne River itself.

FORT ERIE

In 1750, the French built a trading post and stockade at the junction of the Niagara River and Lake Erie. At the end of the Seven Year's War in 1763, when the French agreed to hand Canada over to the British, the French trading post at Niagara had been destroyed.

Captain Montresor was commissioned to establish a British trading post on the same site in 1764. His superior officer, Colonel Bradstreet, oversaw the construction of a row of eleven blockhouses on the east bank and a shipyard on Navy Island. The British also built a rectangular, bastioned fort and a wharf above the site of the present town. The Colonel named the new British garrison Fort Erie.

A community grew up around the garrison and in 1781 a survey of the site was made. In 1800 the first regular ferry service was started between Fort Erie and Black Rock, New York. By 1807, the hamlet had twenty-five houses occupied by such families as the Baxters, Hirrots, Pounds and Sherks.

Galinee, an early explorer in company with Father Dollier de Casson, visited this district nearly three centuries ago. In his diary he astutely described the district when he termed it, "the earthly Paradise of Canada."

"There is," he wrote, " no more beautiful region in all Canada. The woods are open, interspersed with beautiful meadows, watered rivers and

The old Welland ship canal in the 1890's.

rivulets filled with fish and beaver, abundance of fruits, and so full of game that we saw there at one time more than a hundred roebucks in a single band, herds of fifty or sixty hinds and bears fatter than the most savory pigs of France." Lake traffic kept Fort Erie a busy pioneer port. To accommodate the fifty to sixty heavily laden, oxen-drawn wagons that rumbled over the western portage road, ships and boats bobbed at anchor in the bay as they awaited there turn to come in and load their cargo and any passengers bound for the upper lakes.

Quantity and variety of cargo boats provided a busy and picturesque scene. Outgoing cargoes to Detroit list barrels of gunpowder, casks of ball and shot, barrels of rum and other spirits, pipes and casks of Madeira and port wine, chests of Bohea, green and Hyson tea, woollens, blankets and linens, casks of hardware, crockery, millinery, hosiery, flour and pork. Incoming ships from Detroit predominantly carried beaver and other peltries, casks of ginseng; casks of castoreum (dried beaver glands used in medicines and perfume manufacture), barrels of potash and pearls.

To facilitate the transport of trade goods to and from the warehouse, Monstresor had built the fort close to the water's edge. Occasionally storms battered the stone wall that connected the frontal bastions. The remainder of the fort was constructed of wood. During a wild spring gale in 1770, the water breached the walls and flooded the fort and the 8th and 47th regiments rebuilt a more substantial fort slightly to the south of the original location.

The garrison at Fort Erie saw considerable action in the War of 1812. The American ships Ohio and Somers were captured nearby by the British in the last naval action of the war. The fort was twice occupied by American troops and three times dismantled by abandoning forces. It was fired, mined, and blown up.

The most grievous catastrophe of Fort Erie occurred when a chance explosion of a powder magazine destroyed, almost to a man, a force of three hundred who had succeeded in occupying the northeast bastion in a night attack by Lieutenant-General Sir Gordon Drummond.

The Americans, after holding the fort for six weeks, on November 5, 1814, mined the bastions, burned the buildings at Fort Erie and withdrew stores and garrison to Buffalo. This was the end of war along the Niagara. The fort was restored in the 1930's and is now a museum.

After the war new immigrants arrived – the United Empire Loyalists. Early development in the first quarter of the nineteenth century surpassed that of Buffalo, its American neighbour to the south. This Canadian village, due to its position on the waterway, became a shopping centre for the inhabitants of Buffalo and a main distribution point for products from the district.

In 1857, the settlement was incorporated as a village; it stretched two and a half miles along the waterfront and boasted four taverns, ten stores, four churches, a blacksmith shop and a drill shed.

In 1862, fire destroyed much of the village. The Fenians, Irish nationalists from the United States who were determined to free Canada from British domination, crossed the Niagara Bridge in 1866, and then fell back on Fort Erie in their retreat. During this course of action the Fenians were responsible for widespread destruction.

The village suffered another setback in 1872, when the Grand Trunk Railway opened a line a mile away from the nearest ferry and forced the ferry business to relocate in Windsor. A year later prosperity returned to the district with the building of the International Railway Bridge in 1873 by Colonel Sir Casimir Stanislaus Gzowski. The bridge linked Canada with the United States and created a whole new community adjacent to its location. At first it was called Victoria but the name of the community changed to International Bridge and then to Bridgeburg. By the 1890's Bridgeburg surpassed Fort Erie in population and commerce. Bridgeburg amalgamated with Fort Erie in 1932 to form the Town of Fort Erie.

On August 11, 1927, Fort Erie residents witnessed the historic opening, by the Prince of Wales, of the Peace Bridge, an international road bridge connecting the town to Buffalo.

Early in the twentieth century a number of industries were established in Fort Erie. One such business was Williams Gold Refining, one of Canada's largest refiners of gold. By 1930, Fort Erie had a chemical plant, a steel plant and Irvin Air Chute Ltd. Fleet Manufacturing produced aircraft in Fort Erie in the 1930's. The year 1947 saw the opening of Gould Batteries and Strong, Cobb, Arner Company, one of Canada's largest suppliers of pharmaceutical products.

Fort Erie, since the 1950's, has bustled with the activity of tourists crossing over the Peace Bridge. In 1956 10,350,000 people and 4,250,000 vehicles crossed the Peace Bridge. The operation of this bridge employs a large percentage of the population of Fort Erie. One of the largest horse-racing tracks in Canada attracts Americans and Canadians alike from May to October.

Today, the town of Fort Erie marches not to the beat of a regiment at drill, but to the shuffling and bustling beat of tourism. Old Fort Erie contains a host of relics and equipment of British and American armies. The guards, in authentic period uniform, perform military drills daily in the summer months.

Galinee witnessed the natural beauty and wildlife of the district and its power to attract and charm visitors is still there today.

GEORGETOWN

The community of Georgetown, set in the rolling hills of the Credit River Valley, was once called Hungry Hollow.

In 1820, the settlement consisted of three families growing their own food, making their own clothes, and barely scraping a living from the wilderness. A year later George Kennedy arrived and erected the first sawmill. Many believe the settlement was later named after him, while others claim the name honours King George the Third.

The interior of a grocery store in Georgetown.

In 1837, William and Robert Barber moved to the area and purchased a mill from Kennedy. This was the beginning of the renowned Barber Woollen Mills. Two years later, James and Joseph Barber joined the family business and established a sawmill and a foundry. The Barber family played a key role in the early development of Georgetown.

Originally from Belfast, the Barber family left the emerald isle in May of 1822, and arrived sixty days later in Quebec. The family consisted of a father, a mother, four sons, and one daughter, and they travelled by boat to the settlement of Prescott. There Joseph Barber found employment in his trade as a bricklayer and stonemason. Since there was no building construction during the winter, he moved with his family to Niagara on December 12, 1822.

At this time William Lyon Mackenzie was critical of the government for allowing United States paper to be imported. In 1825, he called a meeting and a proposal was presented to the legislature to award a five-hundred dollar bounty to the first man to establish a paper mill in Upper Canada. A petition was drawn up and the legislature passed an act on January 30, 1826, offering payment to the man who produced the first sheet of paper. James Crook, who was building an industrial center at

Crook's Hollow, three miles west of Dundas, decided to build the first paper mill. He travelled to Niagara and there engaged Joseph Barber as a stonemason and offered employment to his four sons. Crook won the bounty offered for the first sheet sheet of paper. It was argued by his rivals that he won because he started the mill on Sunday; tantamount to cheating because of strong religious beliefs.

Joseph Barber died in 1831, at Crook's Hollow, and his four sons did eventually leave for Georgetown.

By 1869, only James Barber and his family remained in Georgetown. His paper making mill was a new industry that he had assumed responsibility for in 1854 and it produced until 1948, when it was sold to Provincial Paper Limited.

In 1864, Georgetown was incorporated as a village. The next year a town hall was constructed on Guelph Street. By 1871, The Hamilton and Northwestern Railway was opened and a junction with the Grand Trunk Railway at Georgetown was economically significant.

The thriving centre of Georgetown has always flourished because of its commercial and industrial enterprises. During the 1870's many new industries were established. The Dayfoot Company, a tannery in 1843, became in 1892, the C.B. Dayfoot and Company, manufacturers of heavy work boots. The company lasted until 1944. Other businesses included Creelman Brothers knitting machinery, 1876; J.H. Day Paint Company, Hillock's Tannery, and the Crawford Brothers, sash, door and planing factory. William Bradley, an energetic business man of the early 1900's started a small seed trade on a mail-order basis in Georgetown. By 1928, he had established the Dominion Seed House, a large mail-order service for garden seeds with world-wide customers.

In the 1950's Georgetown experienced a population and building boom. Its location made it a favoured residential area for workers commuting to nearby Toronto, Hamilton and Oakville. On January 1, 1974 the town of Georgetown amalgamated with the town of Acton to become Halton Hills of the Regional Municipality of Halton.

Today, Georgetown no longer resembles Hungry Hollow. No one appears to be starving or solely reliant on the land, and there are many more than three families.

GODERICH

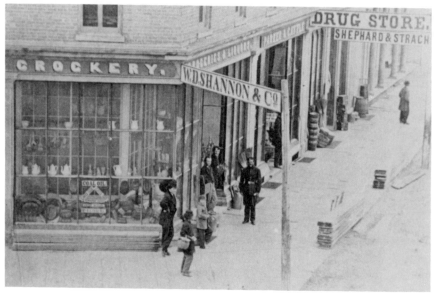

The main street of Goderich.

In the year 1828 they walked from Galt for eighty miles heading west through the bush, led by a man with no fear of the unknown – Tiger Dunlop, the founder of Goderich.

Arriving close to a cornfield cultivated by the Indians, he gazed up to the top of a high bluff overlooking Lake Huron and shouted the command to clear a piece of land up there and build a log house that would come to be known as Dunlop Castle.

The beginnings of Goderich were closely connected to the history of the Canada Company. The company, chartered in 1826 as a colonizing company, was to purchase Crown lands and open up the western portions of Upper Canada for settlers. The lands acquired by the company became known as the Huron Tract.

John Galt was the Superintendent of the Canada Company and considered the father of the Huron Tract and founder of Huron County. Tiger Dunlop, paddling from the south met John Galt and his crew, who had sailed around Cabot Head and down Lake Huron in a gunboat. They met in a harbour now known as Goderich. That evening Tiger served a fine dinner in his cottage, complete with a bottle of champagne. Together the two men named the site Goderich, in honour of Viscount Goderich, then Secretary of State in Britain.

Dr. William Dunlop had served as the Assistant Surgeon for the 89th Regiment of Lower Canada on the Niagara Frontier in 1813-14 and in India 1815-20. Many people puzzled over his nickname, Tiger. This was a man who had an encounter on the island of Saugar in the Ganges with man-eating tigers. Stories such as this one were told of the doctor, who, one day while in a boat on the Ganges River with fellow officers, noticed several tiger cubs nearby. A young officer secured two of the animals. Soon, the mother tiger appeared and plunged toward the boat. Immediately the doctor took out his snuff box and threw the contents in her face. Then, seizing his sword, he struck the tigress a blow that stopped the animal while all in the boat escaped.

The same year that Tiger settled at Goderich, John Galt sent out a group of men to survey and clear the town site for settlement. Galt also made Goderich the western terminus of a road running from Guelph to Lake Huron, which became known as the Huron Road.

From 1838, the building of Goderich took place on the river flats below the bluffs. One exception was the erection of a log cabin by Major Strickland on the bluffs.

Goderich is often referred to as "The Prettiest Town in Canada". Certainly the unique fashion in which the town site was laid out adds to this. The plan of the community is perfectly geometrical. A central park, or town square, is octagonal and eight streets radiate from the eight angles, with the business section surrounding the park. Thanks to the insight of Tiger Dunlop and John Galt, excellent port facilities were developed here. A permanent pier was constructed in 1835 and a lighthouse was built during the 1850's. A successful shipbuilding industry and large grain elevators situated at the harbour added to the port activities.

The year 1866 marked the beginning of the town's most significant industry. Samuel Platt, while drilling for oil near the harbour, struck something else. It wasn't until Platt had drilled to a depth of 960 feet that he struck salt. Before long the Godrich Salt Company was formed. Today, the mine is known as Sifto Salt, a division of Demtar Chemicals Limited. Approximately 1,500,000 tonnes of rock salt are produced annually.

The first member of parliament for Huron was Captain Robert Graham Dunlop who lived with his famous brother Tiger. The Captain represented Huron in the Provincial Legislature from 1835 until his death in February 1841.

A native family journeying to a new campsite near Goderich.

Two candidates were chosen to succeed him. The Canada Company backed James McGill Strachan, eldest son of the Bishop of Toronto, and brother-in-law of Commissioner Thomas Mercer Jones of Goderich. Others chose to elect Tiger Dunlop.

It was a stormy election. The population in Huron was about 6,000, but since only those who had paid for their land in full could vote, the number amounted to fewer than three hundred persons.

One historical account records that by the time the poll was opened Monday morning many had arrived at Rattenbury's Hotel. Axe handles were weapons carried by more than a few and when rival bands met, with banners flying and wearing the colours of their candidates – red for Captain Strachan and blue for Tiger Dunlop – these weapons were likely used with considerable energy.

The genial doctor placed his highlanders around the hotel and they allowed the voters to come in one by one. Votes were entered slowly, only one vote each hour, because if even one hour elapsed without a vote having been registered the election was over and both parties were anxious to give time for every last straggler to arrive.

The results, at the end of the week, showed 149 for the Tiger, and 159 for Captain Strachan. The returning officer, Henry Hyndman, advised a protest. Dr. Dunlop agreed and Daniel Lizars was the moving spirit of the inquiry.

The election trial was a costly and memorable one in which scores of electors were examined as to their legal right to vote and it ended with the seat going to Dr Dunlop, since he had secured a majority of votes from those who were duly qualified to exercise their franchise. As one historian wrote in 1848, "Tiger's warm-heartedness and his personal interest in the settlers made him by all odds the most popular man in Huron County in the eighteen thirties".

Since the 1870's Goderich has been a favoured lakeside resort and its popularity with vacationers and tourists continues today. Modern-day Goderich is a beautiful and prosperous town with many industries. The Canadian Salt Company Limited, Dominion Road Machinery, Goderich Manufacturing, Shaeffer Pen, Sifto Salt, and Upper Lakes Shipping Limited are a few of the leading employers and together they provide a strong economic base.

Most visitors to Goderich take in Historic Huron Gaol. In use from 1842 to 1972, this elegant, three-storey, octagonal stone structure is now a museum. The marine museum is another attraction; it is the wheelhouse from a Great Lakes freighter and surrounding the wheelhouse are steamboat artifacts – a lifeboat, anchors and chains and other items.

The foresight of the founders of Goderich was keen. It is indeed an excellent port, the largest one on the Canadian side of Lake Huron and it has natural resources and abundant natural beauty.

GRAND BEND

Dance once again along the windswept shores; remember moonlit strolls on the sidewalks made from sand; reach inside the silence of the memories of romance; and listen for the melodies of waves that wash to shore; this is the place of summer paradise known once as Brewster Mills and today as Grand Bend.

Grand Bend was and still is the summer resort of Lake Huron. The history of this village, where the mouth of the Ausable River meets the lake, is closely tied to the meandering course of the river.

Prior to the settlement of Brewster Mills, the Ausable River did not always flow into Lake Huron at Grand Bend. Originally, the river flowed to a point 200 yards short of the lake, then took an abrupt bend and coursed thirteen miles parallel to the lake before it emptied into Lake

Grand Bend as it appeared in the 1930's.

Huron at Port Franks.

A man by the name of Brewster arrived at the present site in 1832 and built a mill at the point of this grand bend in the river. As a settlement grew up around the mill, the pioneers named their home Brewster Mills.

In 1845, a large group of French settlers arrived when famine in Quebec uprooted them. They referred to the place as "Aux Croches", meaning crooked tongs, to describe the crooked course of the river. The French Canadians were skilled axemen and they helped to develop a thriving lumber industry and when that was depleted the village turned to fishing for its revenue. The community had two stores and a hotel built by J. Brennar by this time.

From the beginning settlers had complained that the mill caused the river to flood their farm land. In the 1840's settlers sought legal action to prevent Brewster from continuing his milling business, but to no avail. In 1860, exasperated, the pioneers marched to the mill and destroyed the dam. The mill itself was swept away in the subsequent flood – just retribution!

A new name was required since Brewster's Mill had been destroyed, and Grand Bend was the best description of the location. Shortly therafter, the settlers realized that the flooding was a result of the course of the river and that it would continue unless the river itself was rerouted.

Their strategy was to build a straight canal that cut across the series of loops in the river's natural course, from the village of Port Franks to the loop of the river at Grand Bend. This engineering project resulted in failure; the natural harbour at Port Franks was destroyed and Ausable itself almost stopped flowing completely. In 1891, the course of the river was changed again. This time a channel was successfully constructed from the bend in the river to the lake.

Originally, Grand Bend was part of Huron County. During the years of the general repeal of the Canada Temperance Act in Ontario, Huron County remained "dry". The businessmen of Grand Bend felt the temperance movement would irreparably damage their tourist trade and they seceded to Lambton County because of the laws. Since Lambton was a "licensed" county, Grand Bend became even more popular as a resort and as a social gathering spot for residents and tourists from those surrounding counties that remained "dry".

Famous for its sunsets and its vast sand beach, Grand Bend has remained a summer vacation paradise. The romantic setting among pine trees and sandy hills continues to cater to the hearts of each new generation of vacationers.

✹

GRIMSBY

As they make their way up the mountain a stream spilled over very dark rocks, a stream surrounded by hemlock, spruce and other magnificent trees. This stream pushed across a long range of mountains and flowed, with a gentle fall, into the plain and on, to empty itself into the lake. Those who settled here, beneath the mountain, called this place of beauty The Forty.

The first settlers were United Empire Loyalists who fled the states after the American Revolution. Colonel Robert Nelles, a loyalist from the Mohawk Valley in New York State, arrived at the mouth of The Forty Mile Creek in 1788. A year later he built a stately colonial manor and called it Lakelawn, because of the stretch of pasture from the house to the shore of Lake Ontario. This home is now an historic site.

Young couples enjoying a Sunday afternoon.

From 1784 to 1790, Loyalists continued to immigrate in great numbers to the Niagara Pennisula. Most of the land was already occupied along the Niagara River and so a large number of them, about 400, continued westward and settled at The Forty. Early family names were the Pettits, the Carpenters, the Muirs, the Nixons and the Smiths. The inhabitants of The Forty made history on April 5, 1790, when they held the earliest known session of municipal government in Ontario.

In February of 1812, the United States Congress ordered the creation of a volunteer army of 50,000 men. Four months later war was declared with Great Britain.

It was sobering to consider the possibility of thousands of Canadian inhabitants joining the American invaders and taking up arms against the British government.

On July 11, 1812, General Hull and 2,500 American troops camped at Fort Detroit, across from Amherstburg to prepare for an attack. On the opposite shore 100 British regulars, 300 militia and 150 natives led by Tecumseh waited patiently to defend their country.

War reached The Forty on June 8, 1813, when American forces retreated from the Battle of Stoney Creek to their settlement. The British flotilla under the command of James Lucas Yeo, was waiting for them. Bombarded by the British and attacked by natives and militia, the Americans were forced to retreat. A plaque now stands at the Grimsby Waterworks Park to commemorate the Battle of The Forty.

A post office opened in 1816, and the settlement received a new name, Grimsby, after the city of Grimsby in Lincolnshire, England.

The Great Western Railway reached Grimsby by 1854, bringing a period of prosperity to the village. Since Grimsby was located in the centre of one of Canada's major fruit growing areas, the community became known as the Garden of Canada.

The Grimsby Park, originally known as the Ontario Methodist Camp Meeting ground, was the site of huge temperance meetings, beginning in 1859. On a piece of land kindly donated by John Beamer Bowslaugh, the Methodists erected about seventy cottages and a small Grand Trunk Railway Station was opened. It wasn't long before this spot became a popular vacation community, complete with post office, a barbershop, butcher shop, an ice cream parlour, a bookstore, a grocery, a drugstore and two hotels. Accessible by road and rail, the park could also be reached by water. A steamer arrived daily bringing passengers from Toronto. In 1888, a new auditorium entitled "The Temple", was constructed in the center of the park. For many years great inspirational and educational meetings were held in this auditorium.

Grimsby was incorporated as a village in 1876, when its population reached about 600. The business section of the community was made up of three merchants, two butchers, three blacksmiths, two carriage makers and a harness maker.

Since the turn of the century, Grimsby has developed into an industrial centre. The village was incorporated as a town in 1922 with Charles T. Farrell as the first mayor. In the following years many new industries were established. Included here are Niagara Packers Limited, which made Grimsby its headquarters in 1932, and Grimsby Stove and Furnace Limited. In the 1940s, Arkell Foods Limited, which produces canned fruits, vegetables and meats was established. The 1950's saw the growth of John Bakker and Sons, manufacturers of furniture, Robertson-Gordon Appliances; Canadian Westinghouse Company Limited; Jason Enterprises, producers of garden benches and ornaments; Williamson Printing Materials; two egg factories, and a winery. Two printing companies, a foundry, and Reyco of Canada arrived in the 1960's. Since that time, Avco Limited, Andres Wines, and Rieder Distillery Limited have opened in the town.

In 1968 the population of Grimsby was 3,088. A sharp increase occurred in 1970 when the town was amalgamated with the township of North Grimsby in the new Regional Municipality of Niagara. By 1978, Grimsby had 15,265 inhabitants.

The stone Shop Museum, opened in 1963 in a shop built by Allan Nixon about 1800, and the Village Depot, a restored 1900 railway station are reminders of Grimsby's past.

GUELPH

Guelph in 1875, looking like a town in the old West.

John Galt definitely had his hand in the development of Guelph as a settlement. He was not only responsible for the first tree to be chopped down on April 23, 1827, he also designed the site plan for the streets. By spreading out the fingers of his hand, he conceived a radial street pattern for Guelph that has not been substantially altered since its conception.

He named the community after the family name of George the Third of England. Many referred to the place as the "Royal City", since no other settlement in the Commonwealth bore the royal name of Guelph.

The usual growth of a settlement was not the course for Guelph. Galt was an employee of the Canada Company, an organization designed to settle immigrants on the land and he brought with him workmen and mechanics, a blacksmith, a shoemaker, a baker, a wagonmaker and a carpenter to create his community.

Relations between John Galt and the Canada Company were often strained. At one point the Company ordered Galt to change the name of the community to Goderich. He was also criticised for concentrating too much on the development of Guelph and not enough on profits for the company. Galt refused to change the name. Hostility continued between

Galt and his employer and once the village was well under way he returned to England to live.

The first store and sawmill were constructed and operated by David Gilkinson in 1827-28. On the west bank of the river, a mill was erected, complete with a cooper shop, a blacksmith and metal working shop, a planing mill and a woodworking shop.

Gradually, Guelph developed as an agricultural centre for the district. Increased immigration to Canada in the early 1830's led to a growth of population for the community. Guelph, by then, boasted a grist mill, a sawmill, a distillery, a brewery, a tannery, five Inns, four merchant shops, a drugstore, four blacksmith shops, and three churches.

By 1840, Guelph was the fastest growing settlement for the Canada Company; two more breweries had opened, as well as another tannery, and several more flour mills. Guelph's first residence, built by Galt and named The Priory, now served as offices for the Canada Company. By 1847, the population had reached 1,400, and the opening of the Brock Road from Dundas to Guelph greatly increased trade for the village. Three printers were open for business and four lawyers and four surgeons had arrived to serve the needs of the community. Dr. Welsh, one of Guelph's first doctors, was nicknamed the "mad doctor". Somewhat eccentric in his ways, he constructed a log house without a door. The entrance to his home was just a square hole six feet above the ground.

The conductors and motormen of the Guelph Railway.

In 1851, Guelph was incorporated as a village. One year later, the first train of the Toronto and Guelph Railway arrived and The Grand Trunk Railway followed in 1856. Also in 1856, with a population of 5,000, Guelph became a town. To celebrate their new status, a town hall and market building were constructed for centralized activities. Its growth remained rapid and Guelph celebrated city status in 1879 with a population of 9,890.

John Galt obviously had a powerful vision for the town. The one hundred foot wide Main Street of the city is lined with only limestone buildings. A special law, that has remained in effect, decrees that all buildings to be erected on the main street must be constructed of the local gray limestone found in the area. In the early stages of development, John Galt reserved three church sites, all on hills overlooking the small settlement. These three churches included the Roman Catholic Church, St. Andrews Presbyterian and the Episcopal Church. The Church of Our Lady of the Immaculate Conception was built in 1876 with the help of the congregation. Designed after a Gothic cathedral in West Germany, it has become a major landmark in the city.

Three separate colleges formed the University of Guelph. It has become internationally famous for its agricultural courses and now carries out the majority of the agricultural research for the province of Ontario. The first college in operation was the Ontario Veterinary College, founded in Toronto in 1862, and moved to Guelph in 1922. The Ontario Agricultural College opened in 1874 under the principalship of William Johnson. In the early 1900's the Macdonald Institute joined the others. During the 1960's the three colleges then called the "Federated Colleges" applied and received university status.

By the early 1900's the city had many large and reputable industries. The Guelph Furniture Manufacturing Limited, at the time, owned and operated more furniture factories than any other furniture firm in the world; Colonial Whitewear Company Limited was the largest manufacturer of ladies' quality dresses and shirtwaists in Canada; the Guelph Oiled-Clothing Company Limited was the first to make rain-proof, outdoor clothing available in Canada; the Aspinwall Manufacturing Company was the largest producer of potato machinery in the world; and the Gibson Manufacturing Company Limited was the largest manufacturer of gasoline engines for farm use in the Commonwealth.

Between 1971 and 1978 Guelph's population increased from 56,606 to 71,349. The city expanded in area as well, annexing parts of the Township of Puslinch and parts of Guelph Township. An industrial park was established in 1957 and today Guelph has more than 120 industries with products ranging from electrical and communications supplies to leather goods and textiles. Guelph serves as a shipping centre for Windsor-Detroit, North Bay, Montreal, and Western New York. The large number of intersecting highways have given rise to the nickname, "Main Street of Ontario".

Many distinguished Canadians have called Guelph their home: Lieutenant-Colonel John McCrae, physician, soldier, poet and the author of "In Flanders Fields"; John McLean, the nineteenth century explorer and author of a book on the fur trade; Major Samuel Strickland, also a Canadian author; Edward Johnson (1878-1959), one of the world's leading operatic tenors; Lester B. Pearson, former Prime Minister of Canada, and winner of the Noble Peace Prize; Olive Diefenbaker, wife of former Prime Minister, John Diefenbaker, and teacher at Guelph Collegiate.

Guelph's original plan came from an imprint of a hand on fertile soil. The lines and curves marked the creativity and the life line revealed strength and longevity. Vision, spirit and hard work were all it took to give body to John Galt's dream.

HAMILTON

It was rattlesnake country – treacherous, yet teeming with life, finely embroidered by trees, rock and water. A wide sandy beach completely sheltered by a shimmering body of water, the natives called Lake Macassa, meaning beautiful waters. The white man named it Lake Geneva and then Hamilton Bay. Five miles to the west the land rose one hundred feet above the water. The Niagara escarpment curved and wound its way around the bay like a snake on the move. Lush ravines and fresh clear streams ran freely through this valley of dreams. Only dreams today, when one gazes below the escarpment and sees towering buildings, busy pavement and barren industry in the setting for the city of Hamilton.

To the Native people, the sole inhabitants for a twenty mile radius in the 16th and 17th centuries, the land provided everything. The Neutral Nation numbered 40,000 in the early 1600's, a flourishing and organized

The Farmers' Market in Hamilton c. 1875.

band of people. French adventurer Etienne Brulé visited the Neutrals in 1616 and again in 1624. However, for the most part, contact with the white man was limited. Plague and famine in the late 1630's caused weakening among the Neutrals, and they lost a strong chief by the name of Southarissen. By the mid-century the Neutral Nation were disorganized and vulnerable to Iroquois aggression. By 1650, the villages with pallisades were broken down and the population dispersed.

The site upon which Hamilton was built is believed to have been the scene of an Indian battle. A burial mound for Indian chiefs was unearthed there.

Robert Land was the first settler to arrive in 1778 and take up land in the valley at the foot of the Niagara Escarpment. Soon, more pioneers followed and a small settlement began to grow and become a centre for surrounding communities.

George Hamilton arrived in 1813, during the war, thinking this community would be far safer than his home in Niagara-on- the-Lake. Although the war did approach during the Battle of Stoney Creek, the settlement remained unharmed.

Mr. Hamilton quickly rose to a state of prominance. He subdivided his farm and mapped out the streets for a city to become his namesake. The city was gifted Gore Park by George Hamilton, which to this day is enjoyed by the entire community.

The hamlet was incorporated as a village in 1816, but its development was overshadowed by Dundas during the 1820's. Dundas was connected to the bay by the Desjardins Canal and thereby was more appropriate for commercial trade, but the construction of the Burlington Canal in 1830, allowed Hamilton to compete as a port and quickly rival Dundas.

The physical appearance of Hamilton in the 1830's graphically depicted a place struggling to survive. In 1831, the village sported one hundred inhabited houses, six taverns, a few shops, stores and many outhouses. The following year a fire levelled many of the businesses, and a cholera plague depleted much of the population of Upper Canada. Taverns and shanties were hastily erected and many men lived at their place of employment. Families doubled up, and most dwellings averaged seven to eight inhabitants.

Sir Allen Napier MacNab (1798-1862), settled in Hamilton in the 1830's and began construction in 1834 of Dundurn Castle – the largest house to ever be constructed in Upper Canada. A man yearning for the stature of a Scottish Laird, he built a regency mansion in the romantic Italianate style in the midst of all the humble dwellings of the village. Later he served as Prime Minister of Canada, 1854-56.

During the 1840's the morality of the community led to occasional anti-vice campaigns. In April, 1843, sixteen women were rounded up by town authorities and placed onboard a Toronto bound steamboat. A number of merchants sold liquor by the drink and permitted gambling

The Cummer Ice and Coal wagon in Hamilton c. 1895.

in their establishments. There was Daniel Tolliver's notorious house in operation, Nancy McDonald and Mariann Ravelle's Bad House, not to mention Mary Ann Lavill and May Lilly's house of ill repute.

With the advent of railway service in the 1850's, Hamilton evolved into an industrial centre. The Great Western Railway, constructed in 1854, carried trade past Dundas to Hamilton. The construction of railway repair shops marked the beginning of the steel industry. Canadian built locomotives, passenger and freight cars, and the world's first sleeping car originated here in that same year.

The opening of the Welland Canal in 1887 prompted manufacturers to move from Montreal to Hamilton, since their goods could now be shipped as far as Fort William on Lake Superior. Three more years saw blast furnace operations begin in Hamilton. Ontario Rolling Mills merged with the Hamilton Blast Furnace in 1899 to form the Hamilton Steel and Iron Company. In 1910, Max Aitken, later Lord Beaverbrook, assisted in the merging of leading steel companies in Ontario and Montreal in order to block an American takeover of the market. The result was the Steel Company of Canada.

Another important industry also established in early nineteen hundred was Dominion Foundries. The company produced wheels and undercarriages for railway cars. In 1955, it became known as Dofasco.

Many firsts occurred in Hamilton during its growth. One of the first automobiles to be made in Canada, the Studebaker, was manufactured here. It was Pete Smith of Hamilton who invented the idea of the white centre line used for vehicle control on roadways. John S. Kendall, a Hamilton resident created the flashing turn signal. In 1878, Hamilton was the site of the first telephone exchange in the British Empire and the second in the world. Hamilton had the first pay phones in the country. The city's manufacturers produced Canada's first sulphur matches, threshing machines, sewing machines, coal-oil lamp burners and cloth-covered funeral caskets.

In 1887 the Honourable William McMaster established a Baptist University in Toronto. McMaster University moved to Hamilton in 1930. It was the first university in Canada to have a nuclear reactor built for research purposes and McMaster has, today, the most up-to-date medical teaching facility in the country.

The population growth has paralleled the economic cycles. The phenomenal industrial expansion between 1900 and 1913 led to annexations of new territory and attracted industrialists and construction workers from the United Kingdom, the United States, Italy and Poland.

During World War Two, people from Quebec, the Maritimes and the West found work in the war-based industries. Post-war immigration (Dutch, German, Italian and Polish) peaked in 1954. Portuguese, South Asian and West Indian immigrants arrived during the 1960's and 1970's.

By the 1940's Hamilton had tripled its population to 155,000 people. Over 450 manufacturers operated in Hamilton and had attracted more U.S. industries than any other Canadian city. The city had sixty branch factories of American firms, such as Westinghouse, Firestone, International Harvester, Hoover and Aylmers. Products ranged from iron and steel to foods, tobacco, hosiery, and knitted goods. Transportation was provided by railways and three steamship lines.

The 1940's also saw the development of present-day Hamilton. Most heavy industries were grouped together in the northwest, while most retail and professional businessess were situated around Gore Park in the centre of the city. New residential districts were built on the mountain.

The move of the Stelco head office to Toronto in 1968 and the construction of a new mill at Nanticoke shook civic optimism. Most industries in Hamilton have suffered from increased energy costs and economic recessions in the last three decades and environmental concerns are high but it remains a working-man's city. Unionized conditions are prevalent and currently these unions have a membership nearing one-third the total work force of Hamilton.

Today Hamilton is the largest inland port in the country and produces over half of Canada's steel output. Almost fifty percent of the labour force work in more than 500 manufacturing plants and forty percent of the industry is primarily engaged in steel manufacture.

Hamilton continues to reign as a highly industrial centre surrounded not by a pallisade, but by factories, rock and water.

A roof-top view of Gores Park.

KINCARDINE

The waterfront at Kincardine.

The year was 1848. Two men, Allan Cameron and William Withers, embarked from a schooner and set up camp on the beach near the river. They called this place, Penetangore, a corruption of the Indian name Na-Benem-tan-gauh, meaning "the river with the sand on one side." Today it is called Kincardine in honour of James Bruce, Earl of Elgin and Kincardine, General of Canada, 1847-1854.

Withers and Cameron erected a log house which Mr. Cameron opened as a hotel. A few pioneers joined them that summer and a settlement was started on the flats by the present-day harbour and beach.

The need for a grist mill was keenly felt by the settlers who raised the first harvests of grain in the county of Bruce. William Sutton constructed a dam across the north branch of Penetangore River and built a mill at what is now known as Sutton's Hollow. The mill stones were ordered but, unfortunately, on the day they arrived, a sudden storm washed away the sand on which they had been unloaded, and they disappeared into Lake Huron. Undaunted, Mr. Sutton purchased another pair of stones and by 1852 he had the county's first grist mill in operation.

It wasn't until 1856 that the market square was logged and burned. Princess Street was cleared but a good sugar bush still flourished where South Street is today and where the water tower stands there were giant hemlocks. The river, instead of flowing straight out into the lake as it now does, wound through town with a sharp bend to the south, and then ran parallel to the beach for about three hundred yards. This crooked course meant many bridges in the town.

During the first quarter of a century Kincardine became the chief centre of trade for a large section of territory, extending back as far as the Elora Road, and further when sleighing was good. In 1858, a brewery for lager beer was built and operated by Huether and Schownay on Queen Street North. A distillery owned by Henry and Walker was situated where the lighthouse now stands.

A harbour was started in 1855, and a breakwater was constructed of cribs of timber filled with stone. The power of the storms on Lake Huron had been underestimated and the breakwater was washed away in only a few months. It wasn't until 1856 that work commenced on the construction of two parallel piers one hundred feet apart at the mouth of the river. The pier on the north side was 540 feet long and the one on the south side was 190 feet long. They still stand today.

A fishing industry was established at Kincardine in the 1850's and by 1866, six boats sailed each morning from the harbour to lift and set their nets. Fish were plentiful and sizeable in Lake Huron at that time. In July of 1875 Samuel Splan caught a salmon-trout weighing 74 pounds and Charles Splan, in August of 1883, caught a whitefish that weighed 19 pounds. The fishing industry flourished until lamprey eels interfered with the trout population in Lake Huron.

Large deposits of salt were discovered in 1868 and the Kincardine Salt Prospecting and Manufacturing Company was formed. The first salt well was 1050 feet down and located north of the harbour. A second well was located south of the harbour. The separation process involved wood-fired boilers that were very costly to run and the company was forced to close down after a few years.

In the 1870's the Wellington, Grey and Bruce Railway built an extension northward to Kincardine from Palmerston. In 1875 Kincardine was incorporated into a town and by 1908 it had a hospital and a library.

Many of the industries that operated in the early 1900's have since closed. A Wicker Factory was once located on Queen Street and specialized in cane-bottom chairs. The Circle Bar Knitting Company Limited was organized in 1915 to manufacture men's and women's hosiery. Experienced female operators were brought from England. It was known later as the Botany Spinners Limited. After several years of operation the plant was sold and the company was moved to Toronto.

New businesses arrived to replace the old. The Malcolm Furniture Company, owned and operated by the Malcolm family, made wings for Mosquito Bombers during War World Two but for the most part made

A trapper and his Native wife.

household furniture and cabinets for radios and televisions. The Hunter Bridge and Boiler Company made much of the steel used in bridges in the surrounding countryside. They also made the first rotary snow-plough used in the Canadian West. During World War One, they operated a shell-factory which was later torn down. The business is still carried on by Secord Hunter.

During the 1960's, Forenta Manufacturing opened up in Kincardine specializing in the manufacturing of dry cleaning and pressing machines. The Mahood Lumber Company, dating back to 1919, is still retailing building materials. The Kincardine Creamery and Powdered Milk Company operated from 1934 to 1946 as a dairy and a creamery and later began to make butter and powdered milk.

Kincardine has a distinct Scottish community that faithfully celebrates Robbie Burns day by piping in the haggis for a midnight feast after an evening of fun and dance. A beautiful tartan shop imports the regular and dress plaids for all the known clans and it is a special and unusual treat to peruse their wares.

When Ontario Hydro built the Bruce Nuclear Power Station at Douglas Point in the 1970's, there was considerable economic impact on the town. Employment opportunities were abundant and business opportunities increased to meet the needs of the larger community. Some older businesses like Chapman's Dry Goods Store closed their doors but new plazas sprang up to fill demands.

A large hydroponic greenhouse business emerged as a by-product of the nuclear plant. Thousands of gallons of heated water have been rerouted to supply this new enterprise. With each new industry that arrives, new jobs, and new horizons come into view for Kincardine.

KINGSVILLE

The story of Kingsville begins in the 1700's with the arrival of the French to the shores of Pigeon Bay. They chose this site on Lake Erie for its proximity to the French trading post at Detroit. Following the American Revolution, the British government directed the United Empire Loyalists to the area. Few families remained during the 1780's, since the government had yet to determine a method for granting land. Not until 1788 was Upper Canada divided into four districts and surveys commenced.

Thomas Curtis was the first recorded settler in the Kingsville district. Andrew Ulch arrived in the 1790's and built a grist mill, which was to be Kingsville's first industry.

By 1840, Kingsville consisted of a small cluster of stores and mills. It was Andrew Stewart and John Herrington who assisted greatly in the development of the community by offering their land for settlement. Stewart even proposed to name the hamlet after the first person to build a house on his property. In 1843, Colonel James King took him up on his offer and Kingsville became the name of the village.

By 1867, the village had become the lake port for the surrounding township, boasting a population of 500. Kingsville expanded rapidly after the completion of the Lake Erie and Detroit Railway in 1889.

One of the leading figures in Kingsville during this period was Hiram Walker and son. During the late nineteenth century, they drilled wells near the village to tap the natural gas resources in the area. This new and economical source of power encouraged great development in industry. In 1895, an evaporating plant was operating along with a box factory, bicycle factory, broom manufacturer, two carriage works, a pump factory, a glass factory and a grain elevator. The Kingsville carding mill, owned by

Jack Miner admiring one of his Canada Geese.

J.E. Brown and J.W. Bird, had become famous for manufacturing the Ave Saxony Blankets, blankets in great demand during the Klondike Gold Rush days.

The same year that Kingsville became a town, 1901, the future changed from bright to black. The harbour had filled in with sand and the supply of natural gas diminished. Undaunted, the townspeople turned the tables and specialized in growing tobacco as a main crop. Messrs. Wilson and Bailey set up the first business of drying tobacco and manufacturing cigars and loose tobacco. This industry was the forerunner of The Continental Leaf Tobacco Company Limited. In 1919, George Jasperson founded the Essex Tobacco Company which later became the Hodge Tobacco Company. The Ross Leaf Tobacco Company was started in 1923.

Tourism also contributed to the rapid development of the town. The Hiram Walker family were the first to recognize the potential of this new industry. In 1891, they built the Mettawa Hotel to accommodate travellers and sightseeers, who just wanted to rest, fish and stroll the miles of sandy beach along Lake Erie. The development of more resorts has enabled Kingsville to accommodate the needs of all who venture here from within Ontario and from the nearby states of Michigan and Ohio. Certainly the improvement of the harbour during the 1950's helped to develop a home port for one of the largest commercial fishing fleets on the Great Lakes.

Kingsville's greatest claim to fame is not fishing, but bird watching. This town was Jack Miner's home, one of Canada's greatest naturalists, who established a sanctuary here for migrating Canada geese and ducks.

Miner was a native of Ohio, who moved here in 1878. He probably seemed quite eccentric to many as he travelled the countryside persuading local hunters to refrain from shooting geese. Little did he know that 25,000 geese would thank him by making his property their home. By 1904, the Ontario Government, aware of Miner, declared his farm a sanctuary and this prompted the Canada Goose to become Canada's national bird.

Jack Miner was the first man to band wild fowl on the North American Continent and contributed greatly to the world's scientific knowledge of migratory routes.

Today Kingsville celebrates with an annual Migration Festival held in October to commemorate Jack Miner and the founding of one of the earliest bird sanctuaries in Canada.

KITCHENER

It was warm and cloudy on the 8th of May, 1807, when a large number of Mennonites left Lancaster County, Pennsylvania, on a 550 mile trek for the new land.

Joseph Schneider helped his wife and four children into the Conestoga wagon while the team of sturdy work horses awaited the command to start. Only one man, Abraham Weber, knew what lay ahead. He had already experienced this gruelling journey, this trek along Indian trails across the rain drenched Allegheny Mountains, and over and around the swamps of southern Ontario.

The women and children were forced to walk much of the way through the mountains because of heavy loads on the wagons. Often the horses and oxen slipped and slid on steep grades. One horse was shot when it broke its leg in a fall. After one week on the road, they stopped for a much-needed rest. The men decided to play a game of horseshoes. Daniel Eby accidentally struck his brother Peter on the head with a shoe

The Main Street of Kitchener under construction.

during a game and when they could not stop the bleeding, two men travelled fourteen miles to a doctor. After treatment and several days of rest, Peter mended and the group of pioneers continued on their quest.

Many residents of New York State viewed the Mennonites with distrust and contempt for heading to British territory. If the New Yorkers had known about the half-barrel of gold and silver in one of the wagons, the Mennonites might have been attacked and lost their savings – their guarantee for purchase of new land.

They crossed the Niagara River by a flat-bottomed scow at Black Rock, now a part of Buffalo. At Niagara Falls only one house was visible. At Niagara-on-the-Lake they discovered quite a large settlement. Following an old Indian trail below the escarpment about three miles from Lake Ontario, they eventually reached the busy port of Dundas. Here they replenished their supplies and turned northwest.

On Sunday June 21, 1807, they stopped near some sand dunes, and settled there. The Eby's, the Erbs, the Schneider's, the Weber families and the hardy band of travellers offered their prayers of thanks for a safe arrival and then embarked on the building of a settlement.

The massive sand dunes, which were a source of wonderment to these pioneers, dominated what is now downtown Kitchener and covered an area from present day King Street to Courtland Avenue. Like rolling waves on the ocean, the dunes flowed eastward from Queen Street past

Madison. The old Preston Road, now called King Street, was swamp from Ontario Street west and had a creek running from present-day Wellington Street South to Victoria Park. The settlers named their new home Sand Hills.

Samuel Eby quickly made friends with the local Indians. This friendship helped to bring natives and whites closer together, and established a beneficial trade and barter system for fish, fowl and wildlife. He was known as Indian Sam and he soon mastered the native language and assumed the role of emissary minister and instructor. He taught the Indians new methods of gardening and interpreted the language and customs of their new neighbours.

The Mennonites soon changed the name of their village to Ebytown in honour of Benjamin Eby, a man who had become a Mennonite minister in 1809, and a Bishop of the church in 1812.

During the 1830's, Ebytown saw the arrival of new settlers directly from Germany. The Pennsylvania pioneers were mostly farmers, the Germans, on the other hand, were tradesmen and shopkeepers. In a short time the settlement began to take on a new appearance and soon many residents felt that a more cosmopolitan name was needed. To ensure the community's commercial and industrial future, the name was changed from Ebytown to Berlin.

1840 saw George Rebscher and the founding of the first lager beer brewery in Canada; 1841 was the year for a post office to be established; 1846 gave rise to a population of four hundred; 1854 saw Berlin incorporated as a village. The nineteenth century in this town known as Busy Berlin was a continuation and expansion of industrial growth.

It was a busy time. Frederick Rickerman built one of the largest windmills in Canada; Jacob V. Shantz and Company was the largest button manufacturer in North America. The Breithaupt Leather Company Ltd was a leader in the tanning business. The Mennonite Farmers Market, first established in 1869, continued to expand. Coal oil lamps lit by the constable supplied light for pedestrians at night and many citizens stepped into the limelight to play a vital role in Kitchener's history.

One such citizen was Homer Watson, an artist, who, at the age of twenty-four, had his painting "The Pioneer Mill" accepted for the annual Exhibition of the Society of Artists. The work was purchased by Governor General Lorne and Princess Louise and then presented to Queen Victoria who remarked "could you get me another?". His work still hangs in Windsor Castle. Homer Watson held the position of President of the Royal Canadian Academy from 1918 to 1922.

During this time John Metz Schneider, laid off work from the button factory with an injured hand, took his savings and bought a pig. He set about carving out a business – sausage was his game and Schneider was his name. From 1890 to 1893, he kept his job at the button factory and sold sausage door to door. Ultimately he constructed a retail store next to his home. Still cautious, however, he insisted that his plant be built in the form of a house in case it failed. Business didn't fail, and by 1895 his growing clientele soon began to ask for different sausage varieties.

Fortunately, Wilhelm Rohleder, a German immigrant and experienced sausagemaker came looking for a job. He remained with the company for forty-five years. As time passed, J.M. welcomed his four sons into business and the Schneider fortune continued to grow. Today J.M. Schneider is one of the largest meat-packing industries in the country.

By 1907 the Berlin population had reached 15,000 but it did not apply for city status until 1912. It felt the effects of the war years more than most Canadian cities because the local newspapers were no longer allowed to publish in German and the German language was seldom spoken on the streets or in the stores. By 1916, a bitter controversy had begun over the city's name and by the end of the war the new name, Kitchener, was accepted. In 1919, an attempt was made to return to the name Berlin, but it was voted down and it has been known as Kitchener ever since.

A new city hall was built in 1923 to serve Kitchener's 25,000 people. Rapid expansion prompted Kitchener to be one of the first cities in Canada to make an overall city plan. It was completed in 1925. By 1939, with a population of 33,450 Kitchener had 127 manufacturing plants supplying the Canadian and international market. By 1954 there were nine major shoe factories in the city and the city was the Canadian leader in the manufacture of shoes, furniture, buttons, rubber goods, shirts and in the field of meat-packing and hide-tanning.

Kitchener expanded with the annexation of 3,700 acres in 1958 and another 739 acres in 1963. The city was honoured in 1963 as Canada's City of the Year. By 1966 the population had reached 91,321 and it was reputed to have the best-organized growth of any city in Canada. Projects undertaken in this decade included the construction of the Conestoga Expressway, the Kitchener Downtown Redevelopment Program, and the building of a Civic Centre.

Kitchener, as one of Canada's most highly industrialized cities, offers many employment opportunities in a wide spectrum of jobs.

One of Kitchener's most famous residents was Mackenzie King, Canada's tenth Prime Minister. His boyhood years were spent here and later he married William Lyon Mackenzie's daughter. His home, Woodside, in now a National Historic site.

Tourist sites abound in Kitchener. Of special interest is Heritage Crossroads, a sixty acre site featuring twenty-seven historic buildings including a museum, a church, a school, a store, a railway station and an excellent collection of Indian, Mennonite and Scottish artifacts. Throughout the season there are special events, festivals, exhibits and concerts. The Joseph Schneider House is also open to the public. This Pennsylvania German Mennonite Home, restored to the 1850's period, exemplifies the life of one of the area's first and foremost pioneers.

Now, almost 200 years since its inception, the city of Kitchener, once a wave of sand dunes is instead a growing metropolis, a wave of industry and commerce that strongly reflects its origins in its markets and the flavour of its shops.

Lion's Head

The early settlers first called this place of rock and water Point Hangcliff. On Isthmus Bay, along a shoreline of sandy beach shadowed by massive cliffs, a group of hardy pioneers chiseled out a village. On a headland near the village site a huge rock formation, that resembled a lions head, watched over the land. The new residents were so inspired by this unusual rock carving that they changed the name of the settlement to Lion's Head. Down the meandering coastline twenty-two miles, sat the village of Wiarton.

George Moore, Richard Tuckaberry and John Richardson were among the first to settle here in 1871. Frank Stewart, a lumberman, soon arrived and opened a store and when a post office was established in 1875 he became the first postmaster. In those days the few existing roads were in deplorable condition and residents were forced to travel by water to points south. To accommodate the vessels calling at Lion's Head, a wharf was built in 1885.

The natural rock formations and the famous Bruce Trail, which passes through this part of the peninsula, attract a host of tourists to

The "City of Dover" that once carried passengers and freight between Midland and Parry Sound.

Lion's Head each year. The caves along Georgian Bay are a major attraction to tourists and no history of this district would be complete without mention of Bruce's Cave. Many stories have been written about the so-called hermit Bruce, who gave his name to a large cave about one mile east of Oxenden.

He was a man of mystery, partly because he refused to talk about his past; he lived alone on lot 13, concession 25, where the cave is situated. He bought this land from the Indian Lands Department because it was part of the Peter Jones Indian Reserve; later, he sold out and built a log cabin beside a spring not far from the cave.

Bruce arrived from Scotland to work the Bruce Mines on the north shore, and gave these mines his name. He was a military man. Supposedly, he had been in the British army and had deserted. One true story tells how he was once buried alive in Bruce Mines. The foreman thought Bruce was dead and ordered the men to dig him out but without any need to hurry. Bruce, still alive, was able to hear these orders and when finally released, he grabbed a pick and attempted to chase the foreman, but collapsed unsuccessful and exhausted. Bruce never seemed to be normal, and his behaviour constantly warranted attention. He wore a paper bag hat or just a heavy piece of cloth. He also wore a heavy coat buttoned at the neck but his arms were never in the sleeves regardless of the season or temperature. For these and other reasons Bruce was labeled an eccentric and treated as such until his death. His cave attracts many curious tourists.

Lion's Head has remained a small village with a population of under 500. In 1917, the community was incorporated as a village. Since then tourism has been the major source of economy. A news item published in the Wiarton Echo of 1929, reads, "There is quite a nice new industry growing on the Peninsula – the tourist business. There has been a nice little boom in real estate. The hotel at Lion's Head served 77 at breakfast the other day, giving an indication of the growing numbers of people visiting the Bruce."

This boom has continued to this day. The excellent harbour on which the village is situated, the famous Bruce Trial, the caves, the rock formations and the sandy beaches continue to charm tourists.

LISTOWEL

Listowel began when a rifle was swapped for a piece of land. John Binning arrived here in 1852, and bought land from a man named Henry for the amazing sum of his rifle.

In 1853, Binning was joined by William Wisner, the Tremain brothers, George Dodd, and James Barber who took up residence in the vicinity. In 1855, William H. Hacking purchased a parcel of land from John Tremain and opened a general store. This handful of settlers called a meeting and decided to call their new home Mapleton. A year later, however, when an application for a post office was approved, a government official chose the name Listowel, after a town in southwestern Ireland, without any connection to the history of the town whatsoever.

The population had risen to 800 by 1866 and the incorporation of the village enabled the council to raise money to promote a rail service. By 1871, the Wellington, Grey and Bruce Railway was extended to Listowel and Stratford and Huron Railway service to the village started in 1873.

Situated on the Maitland River, just thirty miles north of Stratford, Listowel quickly developed into an important shipping point. As a result, the settlement more than doubled in size within two years and with a population of 2,054, Listowel became a town in 1875. Flour, woollen, saw and planing mills and a tannery were among the industries in Listowel.

The Morris, Field, Rogers Company Limited manufactured Morris pianos and by 1900 the Listowel Furniture Company was founded. Three years later the town became the second largest manufacturing centre in Perth County. To accommodate the needs of the community, the town had five doctors, four lawyers and three dentists in their professional ranks and three banks to handle commerce.

This progressive town of Listowel spared no expense in improving and building schools, roads, a firehall, a jail and new bridges across the river. By 1880, gas lights lined the main street and electric lights were introduced by 1897.

Perth County, as a result of ambitious communities like Listowel, became known as a model county. The enthusiastic and energetic townsfolk not only cultivated the land, but also risked their financial resources to establish commercial and industrial enterprises. The local paper today, The Banner, was actually founded in 1865 by Messrs. Ferguson and Elliott.

Horatio Walker, (1858-1938), who painted scenes depicting French-Canadian life and culture, was a native of Listowel, and a plaque at the Library commemorates his contribution to history.

The town continues strong in its development and yet how little it took to get it started! It is good to remember that good trade relations can actually give birth to a town.

The construction of a bridge on the main street of Listowel in 1893.

LONDON

A rather full omnibus parked near Victoria Park, c. 1901.

Many people find it hard to imagine that the grand city of London once appeared as a pine-crowned bluff overlooking the valley of the Thames. The original surface of the ground at Dundas and Rideout streets was twenty feet below today's roadway. To the east, a swamp covering half a city block was fed by a meandering stream. It is said that an early pioneer lost a wagon in the depths of the bog. This bog was filled in by the 1840's. To the south, a second creek flowed down to where the Hay Stationery building stood on York Street. To the north, a third stream, larger than the other two and just as swampy, fed into the north branch of the Thames, south of Oxford Street.

A tall, gravel-covered knoll stood between the two southern streams and the north course. At the present this is the street allowance between St. Paul's Cathedral and the London Club. From Queens Avenue to Dunlop Street there extended a quicksand bog, a bog now supporting the Dominion Public Building, the former press room of the London Free Press newspaper and the Canadian Imperial Bank of Commerce. South of this bog there rose yet another knoll where the east side of Richmond between Dundas and King run today. In 1859, contractors, clearing a site for a building discovered the grave of an unknown French gentleman with a dress sword by his side. It was also here on this bluff, overlooking "La Trenche" or the confluence of the two branches of the river, that a group of men stood in military uniform. This envoy of King George the Third, led by Colonel John Graves Simcoe with Lieutenants Thomas Talbot, Thomas Grey, and James Givins surveyed the scenery.

The governor's secretary, Major Edward Baker Littlehales, recorded this in his journal: "We struck the Thames at one end of a low, flat island enveloped with shrubs and trees. The rapidity and strength of the current were such as to have forced a channel through the mainland, being a pennisula, and formed this island. We walked over a rich meadow and at its extremity came to the forks of the river. The Governor wished to examine this situation and its environs, therefore we remained here all the day. He judged it to be a situation eminently calculated for the metropolis of all Canada."

Simcoe's dream of seeing this piece of land developed into the capital was not shared by others and a site known to the Indians and French as Toronto was renamed York in 1793 and established as the capital of the province.

It was not until 1826 that settlement took place at the forks on the river Thames. Malcolm Burwell was instructed by the government to survey a town plot in the London Township. Building lots were offered to settlers on condition that they pay $30.00 for the patent and build a small house on the property.

Peter McGregor was the first to arrive and construct a dwelling in the fall of 1826, on Lot 21, South King Street. His log shanty doubled as a home and tavern. He sold whiskey to travellers from a jug over the stump of a tree situated by the front door.

The judicial centre of the London district was moved from Vittoria, near Lake Erie to London when the courthouse and gaol burned in 1825. In London the original frame structure was replaced in 1830 by a brick edifice, while the original building became a school. The new courthouse was a replica of Malahide Castle near Dublin, Ireland, the ancestral home of Colonel Thomas Talbot. He was the founder of the Talbot settlement and owned close to fifty thousand acres of land in the London area. The building was renovated in 1880 and remains standing today.

As a judicial centre, the town grew and Dennis O'Brien built the first brick building on the northwest of Rideout and Dundas Street. It was here that the first barracks were housed. Framed barracks were constructed in 1839 for the British troops sent to Canada to protect against border

Dipping chocolates by hand in the new McCormick's factory, 1916.

raids following the rebellion of 1837-38. These barracks were located on the present site of Victoria Park. The military played an important role during the early years of London. Eventually, the military reserve occupied eight square blocks, extending from what is now Dufferin Avenue north, to the right-of-way of the Canadian Pacific Railway and eastward from Clarence Street to Waterloo. Built in 1830-39, the military complex consisted of thirty-six buildings. A second set, built from rough-sawn lumber and referred to as the "Framed Barrack", was completed during 1843. The complex cost the British Government about one hundred thousand pounds worth $400,000 at the time. Shops were soon erected to meet the needs of the military, including warehouses along a portion of present-day Richmond Street, opposite the reserve and at that time, known as Sarnia Street.

In 1840, London became an incorporated police village. Just as the settlement seemed to be prospering quite well, fire struck on Sunday April 13, 1845. The fire, fed by westerly winds off the river, quickly engulfed every building on the block bounded by Dundas, King, Talbot, and Rideout Streets. Before nightfall, more than two hundred buildings lay in ashes. The village board of police passed a by-law prohibiting the erection of any more frame buildings within the village limits. The citizens of London went to work rebuilding a village of brick. Two years later on July 28, 1847, London officially became a town and six years later a city.

When the southern confederacy fired at Fort Sumter, South Carolina, on April 12, 1861 and began what was to become the bloodiest civil war in history. London got involved. It is said that President Jefferson Davis of the south had friends in London, and drafted some of the clauses of the constitution of the confederacy while he was a guest at Tecumseh House Hotel in London. Many Canadians, including Londoners, presented themselves at recruiting offices to fight in the Civil War. Farmers in southwestern Ontario responded to the need of the armies of the north and supplied the army with Canadian beef. By the time the war was over, many elaborate farmhouses had been constructed around London. This gave testimony to the fact that the raising and supplying of beef had been very important during the civil war.

By this time, London had become quite a city. Carling and Labatt's breweries were well established and Western University was incorporated by an Act of Legislature in 1878. London had become a microcosm of Canadian life – the headquarters of large life insurance and trust companies, the seat of the Anglican Diocese of Huron and the Roman Catholic Diocese of London. By the late 1880's the manufacture of cigars had become a booming local industry. There were no less than ten firms producing different brands of cigars.

Like most villages, towns and cities, however, London at one time faced a great tragedy: the sinking of the pleasure steamer Victoria in the Thames River on Tuesday, May 24, 1881. In those days hundreds of people travelled daily on the River Thames on three vessels that sailed from the dock at the forks of the Sulphur Springs Health Spa to the pavillion in Springbank Park for fifteen cents per round trip.

That day, at 5:25 p.m., the S.S. Victoria left the Springbank dock with a load of 600 to 800 holiday-makers, all anxious to arrive home for their supper meal. The ship was seventy feet long, with a beam of twenty-two feet and had two decks. Just west of the railway bridge over the coves, she capsized. Her human cargo was thrown into the water. Many of the victims were crushed by the boat, but others simply drowned just fifteen feet from the shoreline. A total of 182 people died. Of these, about 125 were women and children under the age of sixteen. Many of the female victims drowned because of the weight of their heavy clothing. Funerals went on for a week. An inquest was held where overcrowding and the certification of an unfit vessel were found to be the causes of the tragedy.

During the 1920's, London lived up to its reputation as "the biggest small town in Canada"; population growth was almost at a standstill. In

Top: The steamer Victoria passes Jerry McDonald's Riverside Hotel near the forks, c. 1880.
Bottom: The remains of the steamer are explored after its 1881 sinking.

1920 there were 181 more people in the city than in 1919 and in 1921 the gain was 503 persons, to a total of 61,169.

On Monday June 18, 1923, the Honourable Ernest Charles Drury, premier of Ontario, laid the conerstones for the arts building and the natural science building of the University of Western Ontario. By 1924 the University of Western Ontario had its own 225 acre campus and more than 40,000 books in their library.

In the field of medicine London has long occupied a prominent position among cities of the western hemisphere. It was Doctor George Edward Hall of the Royal Canadian Air Forces who carried out special research in aviation medicine at the University of Western Ontario. Dr. Hall's pioneering study of the effects of gravity on the human body led to the development of pressure suits for the future of aeronautics and astronautics. Dr. Hall was associated with Sir Frederick Banting who was a lecturer at the Western medical school when he made his initial discovery of insulin in 1921.

In the past London had very little heavy industry aside from two foundries, McClarys and Leonards. The Leonard foundry eventually closed and McClarys became General Steel Wares Limited and then CamCo Inc. until 1988 when the building was demolished. In 1950 the Diesel Division of General Motors of Canada established a location in London on Oxford Street East.

Attractions for visitors today are manifold. The Storybook Gardens, a 350-acre site in Springbank Park, creates a fantasyland from fairy tales and nursery rhymes. Victoria Park, site of the first barracks, is located within walking distance from downtown London. At Richmond and Simcoe Streets stands the Labatt's Pioneer Brewery, a replica of the 1828 brewery, and it features authentic brewing equipment of the past.

Governor Simcoe was right about London and the surrounding area. A far cry from the bogs of yore, it has blossomed into a prosperous city that is vibrant and alive.

LONG BEACH

A Sunday outing at Long Beach on the bay side.

Surveyor Augustus Jones named the beach strip Long Beach in 1791. Anna Jameson in 1837, described the beach as a very remarkable tongue or slip of land which divides Hamilton Bay from Lake Ontario. This land mass was formed many centuries ago by wind and wave; marsh plants and bulrushes grew up along the bay margin and eventually trees appeared. The Indians followed a trail across the strip, but with arrival of the white man, who planted orchards and gardens and built a dirt track for a road, the trail was no more.

In the early days, the beach was a naturalist's delight. The silence was broken only by the calls of loons, crows, night hawks, and canaries; there were gannets, eagles and plovers nesting. As many as 134 swans were recorded in one flock; the waters abounded with fish and game birds; hauls of a thousand or more herrings were common in the spring; whitefish, bass and pike were plentiful. At the southerly end of Burlington Bay near the present filtering basins of the Hamilton Waterworks stood the King's Inn. Governor Simcoe built this large two-storey frame house with two wings in 1794. He felt there was a need for a depot for stores and provisions that would serve as a rendezvous for the militia and act as a line of communication between York, Detroit and Niagara. Lady Simcoe described the beach as 'a park covered with large spreading oaks.' By 1798, several families were established at the north end of the strip (Wellington Square).

On March 19, 1823, the government was authorized to obtain a loan of 5,000 sterling to begin construction of a canal between Burlington Bay and Lake Ontario.

Francis Hall was appointed engineer of the canal project. He designed a seventy-two foot wide canal with piers lining both sides and a protective breakwater to keep sand out of the mouth of the channel and to house the first lighthouse at Burlington Bay.

Soon work began, a dozen men using shovels and wheelbarrows, to dig a trench forty feet wide across the beach. Work continued until the water level was reached and then a horse-powered dredge was used to scoop buckets of sand onto a scow. By the summer, the canal was opened and passage was thereby afforded to vessels drawing less than ten feet of water.

A series of gales during the winter of 1829-30, wreaked havoc on the Burlington Bay Canal. The entrance breakwater and the lighthouse disappeared before the wind and rolling waves, and the piers on the Lake

Family and friends gathering together on August 13, 1900 at Reids cottage on Long Beach.

Ontario side were swept away. An enormous sandbar, forty feet in width, was formed 300 feet from shore, a sandbar over which there was only six and half feet of water. Nine schooners wintering in the bay were trapped until the government took the necessary steps to clear the sand bar and repair the damage.

This quaint setting, not unlike a Mexican fishing village, ended with the coming of the railway in 1876. Suddenly crowds from Hamilton and Dundas arrived on hot summer days, on weekends and on holidays to basque in the sun and cool off in the chilly waters of Lake Ontario. Establishments like Well's Tavern, Sportsman's Arms, the Cory House, Dynes Hotel and Derry's Hotel were but a few of the many oases of grandeur awaiting with open doors to greet visitors and summer residents.

Beach life certainly centered around the entertainment spots. On December 20, 1874, Baldry's Hotel at the canal burned to the ground. On the same site, the Ocean House, a three storied resort built at a cost of $10,000 was ready to open the following May. This hotel boasted a dance hall, music salon, bowling alley, billiards parlor and boat livery. Directly across the road on the bay side stood the Royal Yacht Club. The Yacht Club Regattas were often attended by 20,000 people. Band concerts, ball games and garden parties occurred mostly on the south side of the canal.

Long before Haliburton and Muskoka districts became popular, the Burlington Beach Strip attracted visitors as far away as the United States. Grand summer residences were built by well-to-do Hamiltonians such as Senator W.E. Sanford's wife. Mrs. Sanford built "Elisnore", a rest home for young mothers. The many resorts with their frame facades were examples of society's haunts. The owners of homes had earth brought in to replace sand for landscaped gardens and front lawns. Window boxes became fashionable and nasturtiums grew in the sand.

For many, a romantic evening stroll along the boardwalk to the canal seemed like the right thing to do. The automobile era was still in the distant future. Nighttime brought the sound of music wafting over water. The perfume of fruit orchards drifted across the bay on a breeze. No one imagined that such a time would end, but it did.

It started in 1908, when a number of homes on the lakeshore had to be moved to the bay side to allow for a line of towers carrying electric power lines. The fire of July 17, 1895, had destroyed many of the villas and hotels on the strip, the Ocean House and Grand Trunk Pavillion and later the Yacht Club.

The automobile assisted in this transformation of the beach. The old dirt road gave way to a paved highway in 1923. Summer residences were

Two couples posing for a photographer at the canal on Long Beach.

soon converted to permanent year round homes. The wealthy homeowners quickly fled the crowds and left the sandy beaches behind. The lovely amusement park, situated by the canal, continued to operate and generate a main source of commerce for the beach until the early 1970's. At that time the park closed and the bath-house, bowling alley, food concession booths, arcade and a host of rides, disappeared forever. The only businesses that remain on Long Beach are one restaurant and two gas stations.

Imagine the joy it would be today if the Beach Strip had remained.

LUCKNOW

Drivers stop and take a closer look and pedestrians give it a long stare. But why? It's just a "Welcome to Lucknow" sign. Every town and village has one, so what's so different? At the bottom of one side of the sign it reads:"Drive Canny". On the reverse side it states: "Always Welcome to our Sepoy Town".

In this quiet village first settled in 1856, situated on Highway 86 about twelve miles southwest of Teeswater, travellers ask themselves, what exactly is Canny or Sepoy?

The word Sepoy refers to Lucknow's past. This community bears the name of the city in India which in 1857 became embroiled in the Indian Mutiny. Two Scottish Regiments, the Argyles and the Sutherlands, left the Lucknow area to participate in the quelling of the Mutiny. Winston Churchill, in his book, "The Great Democracies" wrote of this rebellion "The British troops took horrible vengeance. Mutineers were blown from the mouths of cannons, sometimes alive, or their bodies sewn into the skins of cows and swine." He continued, "terrible atrocities had been committed by both sides".

The main battle of the short-lived war occurred in the city of Lucknow and it was this name the Scots who had settled in the Queens Bush in Huron and Bruce Counties used for their community. The Indian foot soldiers who fought alongside the Scottish regiments were called Sepoys. Out of respect for their loyalty and help, their name still remains proudly displayed on the town sign. The settlers celebrated the christening of their village in true military style by setting off twenty-one charges of gunpowder placed in auger holes bored into trees.

The word 'Canny' comes from the Scottish, meaning careful in action, gentle, easy and quiet. The villagers of Lucknow are just asking people to drive carefully and quietly.

The first pioneer settler was Eli Stauffer, a German from Waterloo County who arrived in the area in 1848, and erected a sawmill on what is now known as the Lucknow River. However, James Somerville, who arrived from Wawanosh in Huron County in 1851, is considered the actual founder of the village. It was Somerville who bought land from Stauffer, which he surveyed into village lots.

The village has always been a good business centre. It was a great rail depot but shipping gradually became the business of transports and highways. Farsighted men in Lucknow saw a place for a lumber business in the midst of a thriving community. In 1925, John Henderson and William Fisher formed a partnership in building supplies. Sales and services to beach properties on nearby Lake Huron were an important part of their business and the company flourished. In 1942 when Mr. Fisher sold out, the planing mill, as it was called, continued until Mr. Henderson's death in 1947. His three sons inherited the business and incorporated in 1949 with a new name, John W. Henderson Lumber Ltd.

As far back as 1913, the Siverwood Dairy in Lucknow was a purchasing location for poultry, eggs, and cream for Silverwoods of London, Ontario. In 1923, A.E. Silverwood formed the Silverwood Lucknow Creamery Limited in partnership with some local businessmen. In 1966, a butter making machine from France was installed at a cost of $65,000 capable of making 2,400 pounds of butter in one hour. This placed Lucknow in the front ranks of the centres responsible for making Bruce County the chief butter- producing county in Ontario.

In an old woollen mill J.G. Anderson established a flax mill in 1920. The mill had extensive connections overseas and it became the sole agents for the production of pedigree fibre flax seed. By 1953, after a set-back by fire, a new mill was operating. This time grain cleaning and shipping, especially Garry Oats, were the main mill functions. By 1967 seed-cleaning was the main part of the industry.

Sawmills prospered in Lucknow from 1899 to 1967. One established and maintained a large export business and also supplied top-grade lumber to furniture factories. A second sawmill, known as John A. MacDonald's mill was operated by water- power and was burned in 1966.

The Lucknow Furniture Company was a wood-working shop in the 1880's; in World War Two, it was a stock company making war products under the name of Maple Leaf Aircraft; after the war, it became a furniture factory again; in 1958, The Beatty Brothers of Fergus bought it and turned to making wooden ladders and by 1963, the name was changed to Lucknow Woodproducts Limited.

Lucknow is still a thriving community of light industry and agriculture. The village sign continues to capture tourist interest with its completely unique message.

MEAFORD

A pioneer's first home in the bush.

The town of Meaford lies at the mouth of Big Head River which empties into Georgian Bay. The first settlers to arrive were David and Peggy Miller in 1838. Their log cabin, situated on the riverbank, served as a stopping place for weary travellers. That was how it came to be called Peggy's Landing. The Millers' son David erected a grist mill on a nearby creek but inexperience as a millwright caused his venture to fail and he moved on.

During the 1840's William Stephenson ventured to the Big Head River and built a tavern at this site. The name then changed to Stephenson Landing. In 1845, a village was laid out and named after Meaford Hall, the English estate of Admiral Sir John Jervis, Earl of St. Vincent. The township in which Meaford is located also shares this origin, St. Vincent Township.

One Jesse T. Purdy located here and purchased the Miller property. Jesse's brother Hassard followed hot on his heels and built a sawmill in the village of Meaford. However he had his sites on higher ground and established a woollen mill in the 1850's and planned a new village on his land. His settlement, naturally called Purdytown, became a fierce rival of neighbouring Meaford.

The Northern Railway was extended, in 1855, to nearby Collingwood which Meaford was linked to by steamer and by road. A number of new industries then opened and Meaford, by 1865, boasted a population of one thousand.

Meaford never became a village, only a town in 1874. The immense water stretch on the shore of Georgian Bay contributed greatly to the success of trade once the grain market was opened.

The geographical location of Meaford was and still is a very handsome one, sloping towards the bay for a considerable distance. A wharf, extending several hundred feet out into the bay, was built on the west side of the mouth of the Big Head River. This river, incidentally, was named after a local native chief. The cost of the construction of this harbour amounted to $60,000; $20,000 was paid by the town. Meaford town hall was built of brick and it cost the community $4,000. This was less than the construction of a school, which, when finished, amounted to $7,000.

By 1880, Meaford's business district consisted of eight hotels, six of which were licensed, two grist mills and two sawmills, one of each being run by steam, two tanneries, two woollen mills, a foundry, a machine shop and a variety of shops on the main street.

Over the years, Meaford has had its share of tragic fires and some disastrous floods, all of which have caused some setbacks to prosperity for the town. One fire, in the summer of 1913, threatened to burn the entire town to the ground. It all began in the grain elevator in the harbour and illuminated the sky for miles around. Fortunately, the fire consumed itself before reaching the centre of town. The year before that Meaford had experienced what was called 'The Big Flood'. A power dam, a flour mill, a bridge, a woollen mill, a tannery, a dwelling and the railway embankment were all swept out into the bay.

Following these natural disasters several significant industries were established in Meaford. Furniture was designed and produced by The Meaford Manufacturing Company and hardwood flooring produced by The Seaman Kent Company was the largest industry of its kind in the British Empire. The list includes The Meaford Canning Company, The Knight Manufacturing and Lumber Company and Meaford Steel Products. By mid-century this trend towards industrialization had expanded to include Richardson's Boat Works, George Grant and Sons Limited, Coleman Block and Tile and Amerock Limited, manufacturers of kitchen cabinet hardware.

The hero of one of Canada's favourite dog stories lies buried in "Beautiful Joe" Park in Meaford. It was here that Margaret Marshall

Saunders was inspired to write the novel *Beautiful Joe*. On a visit to Meaford, she heard the story of a dog rescued from a brutal master by a local miller. The book, first published in 1894, was translated into a least ten languages and by 1939 had sold seven million copies.

Thanks to this miller and two others, David and Peggy, Meaford is on the map.

MIDLAND

The region of Midland remained sparsely settled as late as the 1870's when Asher Munday arrived. He inspired the name for Mundy's Bay, an arm of Georgian Bay. Munday wasn't the first white man to settle in these parts. Brule and Champlain had been the first Europeans to travel Canada's inland waterways into Huronia. Jesuit priests came in 1626 to evangelize the 30,000 Hurons who lived in the land bordering Georgian Bay. It was near the present-day Midland that priests, lay apostles called donnes, and Huron friends worked together to build Sainte-Marie. Sainte-Marie was a fortified centre with living quarters, a church, a hospital, workshops and gardens.

By 1649, a shortage of pelts fanned fur-trade rivalry between the Hurons and the Iroquois into almost constant warfare. The Jesuits saw warfare and European diseases diminishing their flock. They removed what possessions they could from the mission, burned Sainte-Marie and loaded themselves and 300 Hurons into canoes and rafts and departed for a Georgian Bay island now called Christian Island.

The townsite of Midland was laid out in 1872-73, following the decision of the shareholders of the Midland Railway of Canada, to locate the northern terminus of their line on Mundy's Bay. The line, at that time, ran from Port Hope to Beaverton. This extension was completed in 1879, when the first train arrived on July 1st at the new station in Midland. Midland had been incorporated as a village only one year before and reached town status by 1887. The arrival of the railroad brought a degree of prosperity from trade in lumber and grain.

The steamer Magnolia tied up at the Midland wharf.

The first mill was opened by H.H. Cook and soon others followed along the harbour shoreline. Early residents of Midland not only looked to tapping the natural resources of their land but also to the water. Frank Bonter was one of the first commercial fishermen to come from Prince Edward County. By the 1880's John and Harry Yates from Peterborough opened a commercial fishing business. Today commercial fishing no longer exists and even sport fishing is threatened by the pollution and contamination of the lake waters.

The first grain elevators were built at Midland in 1881 to accommodate grain arriving from the Lakehead. The grain industry has remained a thriving business.

In 1898, extensive iron ore deposits were found at Helen Mine, eight miles from Michipicoten harbour at the eastern end of Lake Superior. Midland was chosen to be the site for two blast furnaces, built by the Canadian Iron Corporation on the northwest side of Midland Bay in 1899 and 1900. The entire operation was controlled by the Algoma Conglomerate of companies. The iron ore was shipped from the mine to Michipicoten harbour by the Algoma Central Railway and was carried to Midland by the Algoma Central Steamship Lines. The iron ore was then smelted with coke purchased from the Algoma Steel Corporation.

Between 1899 and 1918 the Helen Mine operation produced 2,800,000 tons of hematite ore, grading 53 per cent iron ore on the

The Martyr's Shrine at Midland.

average. By 1918, the apparently endless supply of raw iron was almost exhausted and the blast furnaces at Midland were closed down.

Whenever one source of employment and economic stability disappeared, Midland seemed to bounce back with something new.

During the early 1920's James Playfair, D.S. Pratt and others started a shipbuilding empire. In the beginning they only did repair work, but eventually acquired a fleet of freight boats. In 1926, they launched their first super lake freighter, and allowed the Canada Steamship Company to take over the Midland Shipbuilding Company and the Midland Dry Dock Company.

The Great Depression of the 1930's closed down the Midland shipyards, but by the 1950's the ship-building industry had bounced back and produced the 640-foot Coverdale, capable of carrying 18,000 tons of iron ore or 600,000 bushels of grain.

The main attraction and source of economy for Midland is tourism. Every year thousands of people travel to Midland to tour Sainte-Marie and the Martyrs' Shrine.

This all began in 1907, when a shrine was built to the martyrs, jesuit missionaries who died for their faith at the hands of the Huron and Iroquois near Waubaushene, about eight kilometers from Sainte-Marie. Huge crowds arrived at the small chapel to witness miracles of healing. At the time Jesuit scholar Father A.E. Jones had misgivings about the validity of the location as a site for martyrdoms.

When eight men were beatified in 1925, Father J.M. Filion arranged for the Mass to be celebrated near the site of Sainte-Marie. As head of the Jesuits of Upper Canada, he started things moving. The Jesuits received title to the beautiful hillside across the road from Sainte-Marie. Workmen laboured through the winter to build the twin-spired church of St. Joseph, a rectory and an inn for pilgrims.

The shrine of St. Joseph has a particularly rustic flavour. The vaulted interior is panelled with wood from British Columbia. The altars, communion rail, pews and rose windows are gifts from St. Peter's Church in Toronto. A few panes of glass came from the original shrine near Waubaushene. The fourteen Stations and twenty-six stained glass windows came from St. Peter's cathedral in London, Ontario and the exterior walls are faced with local limestone.

Mother Mary Nealis of Montreal painted the large altar picture which depicts the saints and their struggles. A reliquary designed and made in France contains the bones of Fathers Brébeuf, Lalemant and Garnier. The casket is supported on figures representing Brébeuf, Champlain, Goupil and a Huron Chief. The martyr's names and the dates of their deaths are engraved in the ivory base along with a map of the Georgian Bay mission as it was in 1600.

Canes, crutches and braces hang in the church as testimony to the miraculous cures experienced through the intercessions of the martyrs.

Recent renovations at the Shrine church created the Father Filion centre in the church basement. Here one may view sacred artifacts found during Sainte-Marie excavations – a rosary, a medal, and some hand-forged nails from Brébeuf's coffin. The collection also contains a series of paintings by William Kurelek depicting the story of the Martyrs.

In 1982, Pope John Paul II renewed in perpetuity the privileges granted to pilgrims by Urbar the eighth in 1644. That 17th Century decree is Huronia's first ecclesiastical document.

The shrine church of St. Joseph is surrounded by grassy slopes, gardens, ponds and fountains. Leafy glades embrace the Shrine of the Little Flower, the Indian Park, the Prayer Garden, and the Shrine to Our Lady of Huronia.

Fourteen Stations of the Cross ascend the hill, which is crowned with a covered lookout. The vista looks as it must have done 300 years before. The gentle Wye River stretches to the blue waters of Georgian Bay on the north. To the south are the roofs and smoking chimneys of Sainte-Marie-among-the-Hurons.

Saint Jean de Brébeuf and the missionaries dreamed of replacing themselves with native Canadians who would do their Christian work. Today a dozen native Canadian Ojibway deacons are working in the faith brought here by the martyrs.

MILTON

In the centre of Halton County stands the historic town of Milton. Prior to the purchase of the Mississauga tract in 1806, from the Mississauga Indians, the site of Milton was partly virgin forest and partly marshland with Sixteen Mile Creek following its natural course from the escarpment to Lake Ontario.

The construction of the York Road (now Highway 5), from York to London, helped to initiate the settlement of lands west of Toronto. Halton County, by 1817, had a population of 668.

The development and growth of Milton is partly due to the pioneering spirit and efforts of Jasper and Sarah Martin. At the tender age of twenty-one, they left Newcastle, England on May 17, 1818, and arrived at York in August 1818. Jasper and his family remained in York for the first three years until he received a one hundred acre tract of land from the government, a site that is now Milton. The Martin family moved to this location, fondly referred to as the Sixteen, on October 15, 1821.

A quick-witted and far-sighted young man, Jasper quickly realized the need for a grist mill to service the pioneers of the district. He set to work and erected a frame building and by 1822, had a grist mill in operation. By 1825, he boasted a sawmill, ashery and store as well.

Naturally, by 1830, this small community was known as Martin's Mills and the population of the settlement increased to one hundred by the year 1837. A meeting was held that year to choose a new name for the hamlet. Many locals were partial to the English poet John Milton and by their fancy, Milton had its name. Skeptics suggest it is a corruption of Milltown but the romantic history has greater heart appeal.

During the 1850's, the population of Milton had swelled to beyond three hundred, and to include blacksmiths, shoemakers, masons,

The main street of Milton as it appeared in 1905.

wagonmakers, cabinetmakers, and coopers. Three hotels were in operation and because of overseas demand for lumber for shipbuilding, the
number of sawmills had increased to the awesome number of nineteen.

In 1853, the united counties of Halton and Wentworth were separated
and Milton became the county seat for Halton. This new status for Milton
meant the construction of county buildings and a gaol, completed in
1855. Two years later Milton was a town and construction on the town hall
was completed by 1863.

Even Sixteen Mile Creek changed course to make way for development. Originally the creek followed the natural contour of the land; it
entered the town just below the United Church and first crossed the
street where Metcalfe's garage stood. From there it followed a winding
course and again crossed the street down near the town hall, and crossed
again about 200 yards farther south. The course of the creek was
straightened by means of an artificial tail-race, which later necessitated
filling in parts of the main street to a depth of six feet. A goodly amount
of the original fill used on the street was hand-broken stone, the work of
prisioners sentenced to hard labour in the county gaol of Milton.

The first railway arrived in 1877 when the Hamilton Northwestern
pushed through Milton. This was later followed by the Credit Valley
Railway. A new influx of industry arrived with the rail service. The
Robertson Lime Kiln started operations in 1927 and was taken over by

Domtar Chemical Ltd but it closed in the early 1930's. The Robertson's Screw Company, home of the "socket head screw", at one time employed nearly twenty percent of the work force in Milton.

From 1930 to 1950, the population of Milton hovered around 2,000 but the 1950's witnessed an increase that was a direct response to the construction of Highway 401.

Close to the 401, on the CNR line and the CPR line, Milton is a comfortable blend of old and new. Its businesses serve a large farming community and employ many in small industries and businesses in town.

Thousands of annual tourists visit Milton to view the many historic buildings and to visit The Ontario Agricultural Museum. This museum features thirty-plus buildings and superbly portrays Ontario's rural past. Located here as well is the Halton Region Museum which consists of six pioneer buildings and a three-floor display centre in the barn. Southwest of Milton is the Crawford Lake Conservation Area. Travellers are able to view and explore a unique glacial lake and visit an ancient native village site with reconstructed longhouses. Spectacular to the Mississaugas, it remains so today for visitors and residents alike.

MONO MILLS

The word Mono may have been chosen by Sir Peregrine Maitland, Lieutenant-Governor of Upper Canada from 1818-1825 to name the township and a village in Dufferin County. Maitland seems to have favoured Spanish words when naming townships. He named the townships of Oso, Zorra and Lobo, meaning, respectively, bear, she fox, and wolf. In Spanish Mona means monkey: perhaps he was comparing the rolling hills of Mona to that of a monkey's tail. Some residents believe the name comes from Mona, the name of Chief Tecumseh's daughter, but there is some doubt about her existence.

One of the first settlers to Dufferin County in 1806 was William Franks, a Pennsylvania Dutchman. The township lay north of a range of nut trees, which was, according to the Pennsylvania-Dutch people, an indication of good land for farming. More of his people followed him, among them the Moons, the Rawns, and the Robbins, but sometime before 1820, the Pennsylvania-Dutch left Mono Mills, taking their monuments and gravestones with them from old Snell's Cemetery.

By 1820, Michael McLaughlin and his brothers built the only grist mill for miles around. Originally entitled Market Hill, the settlement changed to McLaughlin's Mills and then to Mono Mills.

The small hamlet was the fastest growing community of the township. At one time Mono Mills rivalled Orangeville, with its several mills on the Humber, its stores, its industries, its hotels, churches and schools.

One of the most interesting families of Mono Mills was the Kidd family. It was John Kidd and his wife Jane Morris who left Gananoque in 1840 and settled on this site. John later became the proprietor of the Albion Hotel in Mono Mills and he and Jane raised six sons and three daughters. His one son, known as Billy Kidd, was born in 1842 and became the adventurer of the family. Some even say he was a gunfighter. At the youthful age of nineteen he left Mono Mills to seek his fortune in 1861, panning for gold on the Colorado River. His account of Denver at that time was that it consisted of a few shacks, two hotels, and a place to cash gold. Not satisfied with the life of a miner, he strapped on a gun and rode as a dispatch rider for the United States Army. The next stage of his career was as an Indian fighter of the American west. Billy Kidd returned safely to Mono Mills in 1872, at the age of thirty. He married Sarah Stephenson and died in 1922.

It was also John Kidd who showed the residents of Mono Mills ,and the settlers of the township for that matter, that romance still existed at age ninety. Shortly after his wife died, John, then in his nineties, shocked the community by marrying a pretty sixteen- year-old girl.

Death was no stranger to the pioneers. In the winter the settlers would bury their dead through five-foot snowdrifts. Immediately after death, the body had to be laid out and packed with ice. If there was to be a wake, the body was placed in a rough pine coffin and surrounded with sealers filled with chopped ice. The Irish, in particular, would throw a party for their lost loved one. They would in some cases place a clay pipe between the departed's lips and provide a drop of whiskey to touch his or her lips.Compliments would be paid to the deceased while they propped it up in the coffin so as to listen. There would be general talk, and tables laden with food, and keening and wailing going on. The dancing and drinking would last all night.

John Kidd's request for burial was to be placed in a glass- lidded coffin in a tomb hollowed from the rocks on the old highway into Mono

Mills. His request was honoured by the family.

Meanwhile Mono Mills suffered a severe blow to its economic base and population growth when the Prince of Wales and Victoria roads were both lined with the Centre Road and the Toronto Line to Orangeville. When the railway reached Orangeville in 1873, connecting Toronto and Owen Sound, Mono Mills lost its dominance in the township. Orangeville took the lead and never looked back.

The prosperous community of Mono Mills slowly disappeared as businesses closed down over the years. Where buildings once stood vacant lots appeared. No one driving through Mono Mills today, would believe how impressive and industrious this settlement once was. The mills and factories and churches are long gone. A few houses and one store still exist at the four corners. The only indication of a time of greater growth is in the cemetery.

NIAGARA FALLS

Niagara Falls in the Niagara River is the greatest waterfall by volume in the world. Split in two by a land ridge, the American Falls are 64 metres high and 305 metres wide, with a flow of fourteen million litres of water per minute. The Canadian Horseshoe Falls are 54 metres high and 675 metres wide, with a flow of 155 million litres per minute. The falls were formed only 10,000 years ago as retreating glaciers exposed the Niagara Escarpment, and diverted the waters of Lake Erie which had formerly drained into Lake Ontario. The falls have eroded the soft shale and limestone of the escarpment by 1.2 metres per year and now stand eleven kilometres from their place of origin at present-day Queenston.

In 1678 Father Hennepin visited Niagara Falls and later published a description of this seventh wonder of the world, now known as the honeymoon capital of North America, a description that was to become world-famous.

The existence of the falls was well known prior to Father Hennepin's arrival. The native people had directed early explorers here before to see these magnificent waters of the Earth Mother. The origin of the name

Niagara Falls, a view of the Canadian side of the river.

Niagara is still disputed by many but it probably is of Indian origin, meaning "thunder of water".

Mrs. John Graves Simcoe, on Monday July 30, 1792, recorded her visit to the falls. In her diary she wrote, "After an excellent breakfast we ascended an exceedingly steep road to the top of the mountain which commands a fine view of the country as far as the garrison of Niagara and across the lake. From hence the road is entirely flat to the falls, of which I did not hear the sound until within a mile of them. The falls is said to be but 170 feet in height. The river previously rushes in the most rapid manner on a declivity for three miles, and those rapids are a fine sight. A few rocks separate this from Fort Schlosser Falls on the American side of the river, which, passing over a straight ledge of rock has not the beauty of the circular form or its green colour, the whole centre of the circular fall being of the brightest green, and below it is frequently seen a rainbow.

I descended an exceedingly steep hill to go to the Table Rock, from whence the view of the falls is tremendously fine. The prodigious spray which arises from the foam at the bottom of the falls adds grandeur to the scene. After taking some refreshment on Table Rock, we went three miles to Chippawa Fort, admiring the rapids all the way. The Chippawa River, is a dull muddy river running through a flat, swampy country.

People cross from Chippawa to Fort Schlosser, but great caution is necessary, the current is so extremely strong, and if they did not make exactly the mouth of the Chippawa the force of the water below it would inevitably carry them down the falls without redress. Eight soldiers, who were intoxicated, met with this accident in crossing the river some years since. An Indian was asleep in his canoe near Fort Schlosser. The canoe was tied to a tree; some person cut the rope; he did not wake until the canoe had got into the strong current. He found all his endeavours to paddle ineffectual, and was seen to lay himself down, resigning himself to his fate, and was soon carried down the fall."

The first white settlers to locate near the falls were United Empire Loyalists. This included members of the famed Butler's Rangers. Ranger Philip Bender arrived in 1781. Philip R. Frey created the first survey of the area and subsequently the Portage Road was constructed between Queenston and Chippawa. This road wound through the Niagara Pennisula following an Indian trail used for portaging around the falls in the Niagara River. It was named Stamford Township by Governor Simcoe in 1792.

By 1790, the region was well populated with United Empire Loyalists, although settlement remained quite scattered. Drummondville was the original village to be incorporated in the township in 1831, and was named after General Sir Gordon Drummond.

Captain Ogden Creighton was instrumental in founding the adjacent village of Clifton in 1832. Monty Crysler built the majestic Clifton House on River Road. This helped to attract royalty to Niagara by providing important visitors with overnight accommodation. The Great Blondin who crossed the Falls on a tightrope riding a bicycle in 1859 and again in 1869 and the famous Jenny Lind, the Swedish Opera singer, were two who stayed at Clifton House. The house burned down in 1888, and was replaced in 1906 by an even grander structure. Unfortunately, it too met a similar fate in 1932. Finally, millionaire Sir Harry Oakes purchased the property and built the magnificent Oakes Garden Theatre.

The construction of the first suspension bridge across the Niagara River in 1848 assisted settlement near the falls. Travellers were transported across the bridge to the United States by horse-drawn omnibuses. Before the construction of the bridge, people were transported across the river by ferry as early as the year 1818. In 1846, The Maid of the Mist steamboats began sailing passengers to the base of the cataracts. The name is derived from a legend about a beautiful Indian maid who, because of an unhappy love triangle, plunged to her death over the falls.

At this time settlements on both sides of the river were connected by a suspension bridge. The village on the Canadian side eventually received the name Elgin in honour of Lord Elgin, Governor General at the time. Elgin became incorporated as a village in 1853. Three years later the village amalgamated with Clifton and received town status. Clifton was selected as a name, since Elgin was already the name of two or three other Canadian settlements. In 1881, the citizens of the town requested that Parliament pass an act to officially call it Niagara Falls.

Meanwhile, Drummondville continued to grow and became incorporated as a village in 1882, and was later renamed Niagara Falls Village. By 1904, when the space between the village and the town was less distant, a union was granted by a special Act of Parliament and the result was the City of Niagara Falls.

Tourism has always been a major industry for Niagara Falls, even back to Confederation when 150,000 tourist flocked to the falls on a yearly basis. Never missing an opportunity to make money, the hucksters arrived here in 1825. They occupied a mile- long stretch of the Niagara riverbank, which became known as The Front. Many local residents disapproved of The Front and felt it was a stain on the landscape that should be removed. In 1878, they managed to exert enough pressure on the government to force expropriation and push the unscrupulous hucksters out. The shoddiness was replaced by parklands enjoyed today by one and all.

Founded in 1887, The Niagara Commission has been responsible for developing and managing 3,000 acres along 35 miles of the Niagara River. The area includes golf courses, a marina, campgrounds, beaches, picnic areas, restaurants, horticultural gardens and designated historic sites. The Parks Conservatory, located in Queen Victoria Park, displays rare and home-garden variety blooms and is open seven days a week. One major horticultural feat was that of Ontario Hydro in 1951. They constructed the world's largest Floral Clock made up of 25,000 plants growing on the face. It keeps time and chimes the hours. Another spectacular site to view and travel across is The Rainbow Bridge named for the perpetual rainbow visible above the gorge. The bridge stretches a distance of 1,450 feet from Niagara Falls, Ontario, to Niagara Falls, New York. At the end of the Canadian side of the bridge is a carillon of 55 bells with a musical range considered to be the third largest in the world.

Niagara Falls ice bridge, c. 1870.

The Horseshoe Falls on the Canadian side measures 176 feet in height and spans 2,200 feet in length. The depth at the crest is six feet. The gigantic rush of water measures five million horsepower. The water of the Niagara first turned a generator in 1873. The lights in Prospect Park were lit by electric arc lamps in 1879 with current generated at the falls. Electricity arrived in Niagara Falls by 1881. In 1906, The Hydro Electric Power Commission of Ontario had as its first project the installation of a power transmission line from Niagara Falls to Toronto. The line was completed in 1910.

The sites to see in and around Niagara Falls cover a broad range, thanks to various Civic groups. The restored Navy Hall, once used by the British Navy is now a museum. Butler's Barracks, and Butlers Burial Ground, have been restored. The Mackenzie House, home of William Lyon Mackenzie and the Colonial Advocate - one of the first newspapers in Upper Canada, have been preserved. Fort George, British Army Headquarters built between 1796 and 1799 and the focus of an American attack during the War of 1812- 14, has been reconstructed and opened as a National Historic Park.

The Lundy House was built in 1794 and the decisive Battle of Lundy's Lane was fought here on July 25, 1814. Now it stands in commemoration as The Lundy's Lane Historical Museum. The casualties from both sides are buried together in the same cemetery and are honoured by one memorial. The body of Laura Secord, the heroine of Beaver Dam, also rests here in the cemetery.

The city of Niagara Falls has certainly changed from its early beginnings to probably the longest strip of motels in the world along Highway 20. But one thing remains constant – the worldwide attraction to view the seventh wonder of the world.

✪

NIAGARA-ON-THE-LAKE

One of the most spectacular and popular towns in Ontario is Niagara-on-the-Lake. Tourists arrive throughout the year, just to walk the tree-shaded streets and experience the atmosphere of this historic town. This town has remained relatively unchanged thanks to years of extensive restoration work in the community. It is an unparalleled example of early Upper Canada.

The first settlers were Lieutenant-Colonel John Butler and his corps of fearless men who fought during the Revolutionary War and engaged in hundreds of forays into communities along the northern part of New York State. They erected a log barracks to accommodate the rangers and, by 1781, a few families were established near the barracks. The settlement was known as Loyal Village or by some as Butlersburg.

The first town survey took place in 1791 when the land was divided into settlement lots for the United Empire Loyalists, retired military men and would-be merchants. A year later, the settlement was named West Niagara because of its position relative to the Niagara River. The same year Lieutenant Governor John Graves Simcoe proclaimed West Niagara as the capital of Upper Canada. He also changed the name of the community to Newark, as it had provided an 'ark' of safety for the Loyalists.

The first Masonic Lodge in Upper Canada was built that year and the Agricultural Society of Canada, the first institution in the province

Soldiers standing, in 1875, in front of a stone building that was once part of Fort George.

dedicated to the advancement of Agriculture, was founded. The society quickly published and distributed educational pamphlets and introduced several varieties of fruit to the Niagara Region. The following year the first newspaper in the province, the Upper Canada Gazette, was published. Newark hosted five sessions of Upper Canada's Legislature, prior to June 3, 1796. After this time, the capital was moved to York (Toronto).

In 1796, Governor Simcoe ordered the construction of Fort George. The fort was designed to replace Fort Niagara, which the British were forced to evacuate that year under the terms of Jay's Treaty. The treaty provided that the pre-revolutionary debts owed to British subjects should be paid by the United States and that the British Government should indemnify Americans for losses sustained by illegal captures. A large sum of money was paid as a result of this treaty. Under its terms, Fort Niagara, on the east side of the Niagara River, was given up to the United States.

Fort George consisted of six small bastions that were connected by a line of cedar picketing and surrounded by a shallow ditch. Simcoe intended the fort to command the Lake Ontario entrance to the Niagara River and to protect the town from American invasion. Many felt grave concerns that the fort was situated too far away from the entrance of the river to serve as a military defense against attack. Sir George Provost, Captain-General and Governor-in-Chief of British North America re-

Left: A picture of St. Mark's Church at Niagara-on-the-Lake in 1906.
Right: Two Native women smile for the photographer.

marked in May of 1812 that Fort George, despite improvements, could not withstand much resistance against an enemy force, nor survive the barrage of heavy guns.

It was during the first year of the War of 1812, that a red-hot cannon ball, fired by the Americans from Fort Niagara, penetrated the roof of the powder magazine at Fort George and set fire to the wooden supports. Eight hundred barrels of gunpowder were stored inside the powder magazine. In fear of a disastrous explosion, most of the garrison fled the fort. One officer of the Royal Enginners and a small party of volunteers climbed onto the roof and safely extinguished the fire before it reached the gunpowder.

What Provost had earlier predicted occurred on May 27, 1813, when the Americans launched a major bombardment and assault on Fort George. Cannon fire from Fort Niagara completely levelled the fort. Under cover of the morning mist, an American contingent of 6,000 men attacked the remaining British force under the command of Brigadier-General John Vincent and although the British put up a gallant fight they were forced to evacuate the area. The Americans soon set about constructing a new and improved fort on the site with trenches leading to the river bank and to St. Mark's Anglican Church.

The summer passed and Autumn arrived. Meanwhile, the British and their native allies were busy re-grouping to build sufficient force to block the Americans inside Fort George. That fall they attacked and by December, General McClure, commander of the American forces, had but one hundred men to continue the defence of the fort. The British advanced on the fort and McClure was forced to withdraw to the American side of the river.

General Isaac Brock and his aide-de-camp, John MacDonald, were buried at Fort George. In 1824, their bodies were removed to a vault beneath the newly constructed memorial at Queenston Heights. A stone still marks the site of their original graves at Fort George.

In the 1930's Fort George was reconstructed to appear as it had in the beginning of the last century. This included a museum, three blockhouses, a guardhouse, officers' quarters, a sawpit, a kitchen and a powder magazine within the gates.

Most of the buildings in the town of Niagara-on-the-Lake pertain to some chapter of Canadian history. The McFarland House, situated on the River Road leading to Queenston, was one of the finest residences in the district. Built of brick in 1800, it served as a hospital for both American and British forces during the War of 1812. Today it stands fully restored to its original design by the Niagara Parks Commission.

The first courthouse and gaol of the Niagara area, erected in 1817, stood on the corner of Rye and Cottage Streets. Navy Hall, in existence from 1775-87, was used as a base of operations for the Naval Department of Lake Ontario. The first Parliament of Upper Canada convened here in 1792. The structure was reconstructed in 1911 from almost total ruin.

The parish of St. Mark's Anglican Church was started in 1792 and completed in 1809. During 1812, it was used as a hospital for the British and served as a barracks during the American occupation of Newark in 1813. The Americans burned the church to the ground during their retreat and it remained in ruins until it was rebuilt in 1822. Today St. Mark's is still an impressive stone building on Byron Street.

The church of St. Andrews, located on Simcoe Street, began as a log structure in 1794. In 1804, the logs were replaced by a frame building. In 1825, the structure was changed to stone and today it is one of the most striking examples of classic, New England Colonial architecture.

In 1906, the name of the town was changed to Niagara-on-the- Lake by the post office to prevent confusion with the City of Niagara Falls.

The town of Niagara-on-the-Lake is noted for its cultural attractions.

The annual Shaw Festival was established in 1962 for the purpose of presenting the works of George Bernard Shaw and his contemporaries. The festival is held every summer and is attended by theatregoers from all over North America and Europe.

A stroll along Queen Street will reveal, among many other things, the Niagara Apothecary Musuem, a shop of 1866 restored; McClellands Store, in operation since 1835; the fudge shop, where you can watch them make it on a marble slab; Graves Jam, fourth generation jam-makers with the kitchen behind the store; and the Prince of Wales Hotel, a magnificently restored inn, which combines the intimate charm and elegance of its Victorian origins with modern convenience.

Anyone wishing to have a first-hand experience of the architecture of the past, to immerse themselves in the vibrations of history, or just to be pleasantly entertained for the weekend should consider a visit to the exquisitely maintained town of Niagara-on-the-Lake.

OAKVILLE

Long before any European settlement, the Mississauga Indians inhabited the north-western shore of Lake Ontario. Their tribal hunting territory extended from Long Point on Lake Erie, along the shore to the Niagara River, down river to Lake Ontario, and then continued along the lakeshore to the Rouge River.

On the bottomlands along the west side of Sixteen Mile Creek, below present-day Riverside Drive in Oakville, they cultivated cornfields. A village stood at the foot of Allan Street. This village site dates back to 1657 when the French fur traders opened up a southern trade route from Montreal to New Orleans.

In 1759 the French abandoned South-Central Ontario and it was not until the American Revolution in 1776 that European settlement in the area began. The influx of United Empire Loyalists seeking safety in the face of revolution created those beginnings.

The Mississaugas surrendered their lands between Burlington Bay and the Etobicoke Creek in 1805. The land at the mouths of the Credit

The Oakville Harbour as it appeared in the early days.

River, the Sixteen Mile Creek and the Twelve Mile Creek were not purchased by the Crown and remained in the hands of the native peoples as reserves.

By the end of the War of 1812, the Mississauga's society had greatly diminished. Thousands of foreigners had introduced frightening new diseases like smallpox, measles, and tuberculosis. With the decline of the game population, many proud warriors were unable to provide for their families and had lost their self-esteem. Their numbers dwindled to 200 and they faced extinction.

On February 20, 1820, William Claus, deputy superintendent-general of Indian affairs arrived with a fat ox, some flour, and a keg of rum to meet the Indians. The Crown wanted more land. The native people were promised food, housing and schooling if they gave up nine thousand acres of land in exchange for 200 acres and government assistance. Not able to read English nor to understand that the government might not care for this land nor for their children, they signed. The Mississauga's left Sixteen Mile Creek to settle on reserve land and where there was once an ancient summer village named Nanzuhzauqewazog, meaning 'having two outlets', a new village grew named Oakville. The name is thought to have come from the abundant groves of oak trees in this area.

About the same time, a man by the name of William Chisholm began buying pine timber in the district covered by the Mississauga Purchase.

Aware of the need for ships to transport commodities, he began in 1794 to build his own. By 1827, he had a fleet of five schooners sailing the waters from Lake Ontario to points on the St. Lawrence.

He set his sights on the Sixteen which was a stream with a sufficiently steep profile for mill sites. Adjacent to the Sixteen at the mouth, the land lent itself to the construction of docks. Chisholm arranged with the Governor to hold a sale of the lands at the mouth of the Sixteen and at a public auction he purchased 960 acres for the sum of $4,116.00.

William Chisholm laid out a town plot and harnessed the Sixteen to make power for saw, grist, and flour mills. By the spring of 1830, the harbour had been dredged and a pier of 576 feet constructed. A second pier was well underway by this time.

The first hotel was built in the winter of 1827-28, by William Young. It stood at the northeast corner of present-day Colborne and Navy Streets. By 1833, William Wellers' stage line was in operation. A steamship service began the same year with the arrival of the streamer, Constitution. The following year, sixteen ships were engaged in exporting wheat, wood, flour and potash. On the return trip the ships brought back immigrants as well as supplies.

In 1836, the Oakville Brewing and Distillery Company, owned and operated by two Scotsmen Hopkirk and Watson, opened its doors on Walker Street.

The opening of the Aberdeen Bridge in 1895.

On December 3, 1855, an excited crowd gathered to view the first Great Western train passing through Oakville. Two years later Oakville was incorporated as a town. Oakville's early growth had peaked, oak timber in the district was becoming scarce and wooden ships were being replaced by steel boats. Oakville was about to change from an industrial settlement to a lavish recreational centre. Wealthy residents of Toronto and Hamilton found it fashionable to spend their summers in beautiful Oakville. They built exquisite estates and elaborate cottages along the lakeshore. The summer residents were vastly outnumbered by the daytime excursionists who arrived in Oakville by steamer. By the 1880's, the steamers were bringing anywhere from 1,000 to 3,000 people a day from Toronto and Hamilton.

Many vacationers held picnics at Georges Square and watched baseball games between Oakville's White Oakes, Bronte's Ciscoes, and visiting Toronto clubs. Everyone delighted in boating, swimming and canoe racing. In the winter people skated on the Sixteen and stood on its banks to watch trotting races on a track laid out on the ice. The Village Inn, on the east side of Howard Avenue was an unusual and commodious summer resort with nearly forty bedrooms and wide verandahs overlooking the lake. It also featured tennis courts, a dance-floor and a dining room.

By 1909, Herbert C. Cox, of the Canadian Life Assurance Company, arrived in Oakville and built Ennisclare, a seventeen acre estate, with stables for his throughbred horses and a polo field. W.D. Gregory built Montacute House which later became the summer home of Mrs. Timothy Eaton.

The automobile transformed Oakville. The community was closely connected to Toronto by Lakeshore Road and in December 1915, it was paved. Oakville was flooded with tourists from Toronto and from the United States as Americans made their way to Canadian cottage country. Gas pumps were installed in front of retail stores and lunch counters and restaurants came into being. The fruit-growing industry and tourism kept Oakville prosperous.

The Queen Elizabeth Way was opened in 1939 and industrialization was inevitable. In 1953 the Ford Motor Company established a manufacturing plant in town. This was followed by smaller related industries and oil refineries. The commercial development went hand-in-hand with an increase in population and the town lost much of its rural character. In 1961 Trafalgar Township was annexed by the town. Today more than 120 plants make up Oakville's industrial community, producing everything from automobiles, auto parts and aluminumware to patent leather, plastics, and commercial baskets. The surrounding area with fruit, dairy and poultry farms add to the commerce of Oakville. Educational facilities include Appleby College and Sheridan College of Applied Arts and Technology.

Admidst sailing races and high tea, Oakville became what some would call a respectable and successful town. A walk up and down the laneways of the lakeshore testifies to its history as those summer residences and cottages still stand, seemingly untouched by time. The harbour remains busy with summer activity, while the main street reflects the prosperity of shopkeepers.

ORANGEVILLE

Long before the first white man came to the Orangeville district the area was heavily populated by native people. The Mississauga tribe lived along the Credit River. To the north in Nottawasaga Hills there were the Petun or Tobacco Nation, so called because they grew tobacco and traded with other tribes. This countryside was one of the main hunting grounds. The Credit River, below the falls at Cataract, teemed with salmon and above the falls, with trout. It is said that salmon runs were so large that they actually filled the Credit River to overflowing. The mills, built on the river by the settlers, eventually destroyed the runs. By the early 1840's, the salmon had disappeared completely. The wapiti (elk), the black bear, the timber wolf, the lynx and the wolverine once freely roamed this territory. Wild turkeys wandered throughout the forest land and passenger pigeons nested here. The last recorded flock was ten passenger pigeons, seen in Orangeville in 1899.

Orangeville, situated at the headwaters of the Credit River, was originally called "The Mills" because James Greggs had erected a sawmill and flour mill around 1832.

Ezekial Beanson, a surveyor, received the first land patent in 1820. In 1844, Orange Lawrence, a United Empire Loyalist, purchased one hundred acres and erected a primitive sawmill on the riverbank. A village grew up around that mill.

Native encampment and birchbark canoe.

Several stories have been told as to how Orangeville received its name. Here is one: When the frame of the sawmill was erected, a Mr. Corbett climbed to the highest plate with a bottle of whiskey to christen the mill, as was the custom. He said, "A good frame deserves a good name. What shall we call it?" An Irish lady, Mrs. Newton shouted, "Call it Harangeville." The bottle of whiskey soared through the air into the mill race and the men after it. And so the tiny village was called Orangeville. Another story, a less colourful but more plausible one, has it named after Orange Lawrence himself.

In 1850, the opening of the Prince of Wales Road gave a boost to Orangeville. This new route ran from Toronto to Owen Sound and Orangeville became a main stopping place for travellers on that route. By 1856, a stageline was in operation between Orangeville and Brampton, operated by W.J. Lewis. Several years later R. Trimble instituted a stage-coach line from Orangeville to Owen Sound. The stage was scheduled to leave Orangeville at 7 a.m. every Tuesday and Friday and to arrive in Owen Sound on Wednesday and Saturday at 2 p.m. The one-way fare was three dollars. The trip by stage from Toronto to Owen Sound in 1867, took a little over two days and cost four dollars.

In 1863, Orangeville was incorporated as a village. The village experienced a great era of expansion in the 1870's after the Toronto,

Grey and Bruce Railway established a route here from Toronto. Orangeville became a town in 1874 and when Dufferin County was formed in 1879, it became the county town.

Today, the town of Orangeville has one of the most historically interesting main streets in all of Ontario. Many buildings and storefronts are architecturally intact, the street is very wide and some beautiful old homes have been converted into specialty shops. Massive and lovely period churches remain well-cared for and the newer shops and eateries have been kept out of the old section of downtown so far. The back streets have gracious old homes in abundance and development has been gradual enough to prevent the feeling of suburbia. Animals may no longer be abundant but an eagle was sighted and definitely identified in 1990 at the junction of highways 9 and 10 and the farmland is protected and still flourishing. An active group of environmentally conscious people have undertaken to initiate considerable measures to promote ecological awareness which is keeping Orangeville on the leading edge of agricultural trends. Easy access to the larger metropolis of Toronto has provided for a culturally appreciative community. These factors have created a blend of new ideas and traditional values that make for a comfortable and viable community life.

OWEN SOUND

One of the most interesting chapters of Ontario history involves shipwrecks. Some of the greatest shipwreck stories originate from the Georgian Bay area.

Many a ship left the safety of Owen Sound's harbour, never to return again. Such was the case of the steamer Asia, built in St. Catharines in 1873.

The story begins near midnight on the 13th of September 1882, as the steamer Asia cruised out of the harbour of Owen Sound bound for Sault Ste. Marie, with more than a hundred passengers on board. Only Christina Morrison of Owen Sound and Douglas Albert Tinkis of Little Current survived the journey.

The main street of Owen Sound.

Laden with eighty-five tons of merchandise and fifteen horses teth-ered to the deck of her hull, she cut a smooth path across the waters edge. It was a clear night with a gentle, warm breeze out of the southwest and steady on her course the Asia headed out of the sound.

The night passed without difficulty. By morning a stiff westerly gale began to blow and Captain Savage changed course and ran before the wind. He headed for the French River. The horses, sensing danger, frantically scrambled to break away from the railings. Orders went out to throw the animals overboard and as much cargo as possible. Passengers scurried to the deck wearing life preservers.

Awakened by his uncle, Douglas Tinkis jumped from his bunk and scrambled to the deck. Mr. Tinkis remembered this, "The storm was raging, the wind blowing a perfect hurricane and the waves appeared to be rolling mountains high. The steamer had got into the trough of the sea and though her engines worked hard the vessel refused to obey her helm. Wave after wave swept over us, each of which threatened to engulf us, until one larger than the rest struck us, and the ship turned on its side."

Miss Morrison had risen about 8 a.m. on the morning of the 14th, but because she felt seasick she returned to her cabin. She states, "I knew there was danger, and I saw people putting on life preservers. My state room was about in the middle of the ship on the port side, my cabin door opened out on deck. At about 11 a.m. the ship appeared to take a violent

The steamer Asia, built in 1873 in St. Catharines.

lurch to the starboard. I climbed up over the ship which was sinking rapidly and let myself slide down into the water. The captain and mate assisted me into a lifeboat."

Mr Tinkis also managed to haul himself into the lifeboat. He recalls, "As soon as I got in I looked towards the wreck, where nothing was to be seen but a struggling mass of humanity, who were clinging to pieces of timber and other wreckage to prolong their lives even for a few seconds."

Three life boats drifted for a short time. Soon two of the boats disappeared in the trough of a hurling wave to later reappear, empty of its passengers.

With no land in view the eighteen survivors of the Asia valued every breath. With every wave, the numbers diminished. The struggle with death had begun. One by one, passengers disappeared in the waves.

Despite the agony around them, Miss Morrison and Douglas Tinkis remained firm. Two days later they reached land, just the two of them about twenty-five miles from Parry Sound. Everyone else had perished. Local natives brought them in to Parry Sound. Such were the shipwrecks of Georgian Bay!

The city of Owen Sound wasn't always a busy port. Situated at the northern terminus of the Garafraxa Road, it was, in the early days, called

Sydenham Bay after Lord Sydenham, Governor-in-Chief of Canada from 1838-41. This inlet of Georgian Bay provided a natural harbour on which a new town was founded. John Telfer, a government-appointed land agent and cousin to Sir John A. Macdonald, built a house on the site in 1842. He also erected a government shelter consisting of two buildings, one for storage, and the other for settlers to reside in while they built their new homes.

Eventually, those people calling at the port began to refer to it as Owen's Sound, after Captain William Fitzwilliam Owen R.N., who charted it in 1815. The new settlement then became a port of call for steamers plying between Lake Huron and ports of Georgian Bay.

In 1842, the government sent workmen to build sixteen log houses for the native people of the area. More than one hundred acres of land was cleared for them and oxen and milk cows were provided.

When John Telfer returned with his daughter Elizabeth, age sixteen, her presence awed the Newash Indians who paddled out to greet their boat. She was the first white woman they had seen. The Newash welcomed them by smoking the pipe.

George Gale, later the county clerk, arrived in 1843 and reported a population of forty people, eight shanties, and six business establishments.

W.C. Boyd built a wharf, in 1844, that was 300 feet of stone from the escarpment. Many of the ships arrived at night from as far away as Chicago. Boyd's wharf was later swept away by a bad storm.

Development of the community accelerated in the 1850's and by 1857, Owen Sound was incorporated as a town. The population had reached 2,000 at that time.

In 1867, the first steamboat, the Frances Smith, was built. This was the introduction of a new industry to the town. To this date, Owen Sound had foundries, tanneries, asheries, and a brickyard. By the 1880's grain elevators were constructed and promised to enhance the industrial base of the town. This was accentuated by the arrival of the railroad. The future of Owen Sound as a major grain transfer point ended in 1905, when the elevators burned to the ground and were not rebuilt.

Owen Sound became a city in 1920, and continued to prosper in the shipbuilding industry, the manufacture of machinery, furniture, vending machines, textiles, paint, and agricultural products. Today many people are attracted to Owen Sound to spend a few summer days fishing or to browse in the downtown shopping area.

The County of Grey and Owen Sound Museum has a collection of the material culture of the County and of Owen Sound dating back to 1815.

Much of the history is displayed in three galleries and five restored buildings.

William Avery Bishop (better known as Billy Bishop), one of World War One's greatest fighting pilots, was born in Owen Sound. Credited with the destruction of seventy-two enemy aircraft, he was awarded the Victoria Cross, the Distinquished Service Order, and the Military Cross. During World War Two he served as director of recruiting for the R.C.A.F. with the rank of Air Marshall.

One spot not to miss while visiting Owen Sound is the Tom Thomson Memorial Art Gallery. Located a few miles from his boyhood home, this gallery is named for Thomson, Canada's best known landscape painter. In addition to a small display of his work, and that of the Group of Seven, exhibits feature a wide variety of art.

From water ships to air ships, Owen Sound seems to have its share of heroes. It has a rugged spirit that matches the rugged land, the strong waters and the whistling wind. This is the nature that welcomed them like the pipe of the Newash.

PENETANGUISHENE

The natives called this peninsula, by the waters of Georgian Bay, Penetanguishene meaning "Place of the White Rolling Sands."

Penetanguishene harbour had long been a base and centre of activity for fur traders. The choice of this site for trading was a logical one since it was at the southern end of a seven-mile land-locked bay.

Governor John Graves Simcoe visited the site in 1797 and proposed building a military road from Kempenfeldt Bay (Barrie) on Lake Simoce, to terminate at Penetanguishene. In 1798 Simcoe purchased the Penetanguishene Peninsula from the Ojibway Indians for the sum of one hundred pounds. By 1814, the road, which actually originated in York, was completed.

Settlement to the area was slow until the final construction in 1818 of a military establishment and this fortification was intended to replace Fort Nottawasaga. Although it was first started at the end of the War of

Downtown Penetanguishene in 1938.

1812, it was completed more as a precaution against the renewal of hostilities than as a place of combat. Large sums of British money maintained the fort and created a market for goods and services.

By the early 1820's the dockyard and many whitewashed log buildings had been built. The military establishment included barracks, officers' quarters, a hospital and the three-storied red storehouse which dominated the waterfront. Two schooners were anchored in the harbour, without masts or rigging, but otherwise in a state of readiness in case war broke out again between the United States and British North America.

The arrival of settlers in 1827-28 coincided with the transfer of the naval garrison from Drummond Island to Penetanguishene after the island had been ceded to the Americans by the Treaty of Ghent, signed in 1814. The stationing of this garrison at Penetanguishene boasted the economy of the region. The military presence of the settlement certainly added an unprecedented sparkle to pioneer life in the area.

By 1834, the British Admiralty decided to leave the waters of Georgian Bay. Since the two schooners in the harbour were no longer seaworthy, orders went out that the ships had to be cut adrift and allowed to sink nearby.

Over the next two decades units of many famous British Regiments served at Penetanguishene, including the Royal Canadian Rifle Regiment, a British force that was specifically trained to staff the frontier forts of Upper Canada.

The village itself grew up around the military establishment, and its population was composed of British military families and French-speaking Canadians who were engaged in the fur trade and fishing industry.

In 1836 the historic St. James-on-the-Lines Church was built, to serve the military personnel stationed here. Its wide aisles were built to allow soldiers to enter two abreast and step in time to their pews. The pews were designed and carved by individual members of the garrison and this was responsible for the wide variety of styles. As the years passed, the threat of invasion seemed highly unlikely. The regular units were called home and were replaced by half-pay soldiers, who supplemented their income by farming.

In 1856, "the fort that never fired a shot", was closed down permanently by the Canadian government. The Provincial Government acquired the property in 1859 and established a reformatory there. In 1875, the settlement was incorporated into a village and in 1882, Penetanguishene became a town with a population of 1,200.

Penetanguishene was a lake port, and its economic well-being was tied to maritime activities such as lumber, ship-building and fishing. During the 1890's the town was at the centre of the lumbering boom. There were four major lumbering mills in operation. The Firstbrook Box Company opened its doors for business in 1867. Their head office was located in Toronto. By the end of the century, the Penetanguishene

The Penetanguishene Hotel in 1898.

operation covered more than seventy waterfront acres and was served by the Grand Trunk Railway. The plant was able to turn out 100,000 feet of custom-sawn lumber per day, and its box-making department used some 700,000 feet of timber every month.

The C. Beck Company was the largest mill with its operation stretching for almost a mile along the Penetanguishene waterfront. Thousands of logs could be seen floating down Georgian Bay in great rafts, fenced by booms, behind tugs.

Early in the Twentieth century the lumber industry ended, because the land had been depleted of virgin forests. Fortunately, Penetanguishene had time to adjust to changing conditions and to find new paths to economic and civic progress. One source of revenue was from summer vacationers, eager to escape the heat of the big Canadian and American cities. The steamer Georgina, operated by C. Beck and Company, offered a three-day-a-week service from Penetanguishene to Parry Sound. It stopped at the summer resorts along the way and promised to convey campers and cottagers, together with supplies and outfits, to any island or destination that they desired. Campers could return whenever they wished within the schedule of regular runs. Other vacationers, like heads of state, wealthy industrialists from Canada and the United States, famous artists and musicians, chose to stay at the Penetanguishene Hotel. Even the Wright brothers, who inaugurated the age of aviation, vacationed there.

Built in 1889, the hotel offered the finest in luxury accommodation and gracious living. Acres of shaded lawns surrounding the resort catered to naturalists and romantics. An orchestra entertained diners during lunch and over dinner, while the sports-minded played tennis or enjoyed lawn bowling. The hotel had its own supply of electricity, steam heat in every room and a dedication to attracting "the annual patronage of the best class of people". Unfortunately, the Penetanguishene Hotel shared the fate of other Georgian Bay hotels, like the Palmer House and the Georgian Bay House; it burned to the ground during World War One.

An important development in Penetanguishene in this century has been an institution for the mentally ill. From the late 1850's until 1904 the barracks of the old naval and military base were used as a reformatory for boys. Then it became an Asylum for the Insane. Existing buildings were renovated or replaced and the Oak Ridge division was added in two stages, in 1933 and 1958. In 1967 the two retraining buildings, Bayfield and Brébeuf, were opened and by 1972 the impressive and modern seven-storey treatment building was complete.

Staff-patient ratio has changed from one staff for six patients to a present-day situation of almost one on one. The mental health operation at Penetanguishene is regarded as one of the best in Canada.

Today the town of Penetanguishene continues to cater to summer vacationers, and curious travellers. In 1964, the Ontario Government announced its intention to reconstruct the British Naval and Military Establishments at Penetanguishene as an historical site and tourist attraction. Reconstruction began in 1968, and in 1971 the rebuilt fort was turned over to the Huronia Historical Parks authority for administration. The one thing that every tourist should do while visiting Penetanguishene is take a trip on the M.S. Georgian Queen. This three hour cruise takes you through the largest concentration of islands in the world.

This "place of white rolling sand" must be as magnificent as it was to the native people when it is viewed from off shore, away from the development of the last two hundred years.

PORT COLBOURNE

Port Colborne, situated on both Lake Erie and the Welland Canal in the Niagara Peninsula, is the site of one of the largest single canal locks in the world.

The first recorded settler in this area of Lake Erie was Robert Richardson in 1802. The construction of the Welland Canal brought the first permanent settlement in 1832. The first village located at Gravelly Bay, was named after the Lieutenant Sir John Colborne and included a few inhabitants in a few shanties, dotted along the lakeshore. The population in the year 1833 was 160. The following year a new village site was laid out farther inland with streets on both sides of the Welland Canal. William H. Merritt, president of the canal company was responsible for this move. He was also responsible for a grist mill which boosted the local economy from sole dependancy on the operation of the canal.

It was during the Fenian Raids of Upper and Lower Canada, that the Welland Canal Field Battery was stationed at Port Colborne for the defence of the settlement along Lake Erie and the canal.

Picking for mussels in the harbour at Port Colbourne.

Shortly after the close of the Civil War another danger threatened peace between Canada and the United States. The danger came from the Fenian Brotherhood – a society of Irishmen who sought to force the British to give Ireland its freedom. The Irish-American members also banded together along the border with the intent to attack the British North American colonies because of their British association.

In June of 1866, two raids were made by Fenians against Upper and Lower Canada. At Niagara, a force of 800 crossed the border and ransacked Fort Erie. Later they struck at Port Colborne where they were met by a Canadian militia of seventy men. Logistical and administrative disorganization caused the Canadian unit to be defeated and captured. A larger force of 1,800 Fenians moved in the Eastern Townships from Veermount, but withdrew across the border after a few days.

The Fenian raids were restrained by the Americans but the government did not attempt to control the Brotherhood. For five years the possibility of Fenian raids kept the border of the British colonies from New Brunswick to Manitoba in a state of alarm.

By 1875, Port Colborne had four churches, a public school, a seperate school, a grist mill, a sawmill, three planing mills, a sash and door factory, a branch of the Imperial Bank, offices of the Montreal and Dominion Telegraph, and a grain elevator. Port Colborne was also the southern terminus of the Welland Railway and a station on the Buffalo and Goderich Division of the Grand Trunk Railway. In 1890, with a population of 1,030 Port Colborne was incorporated as a village.

In 1918, Port Colborne became a town. The population at this time was approximately 5,000. This was the beginning of a period of increased prosperity. A modern grain elevator had already been built along with the largest flour mill in the British Empire which was operated by the Maple Leaf Milling Company. The fourth Welland Canal, the longest lock in the world (1,380), was completed. In the early twenties a new distillery was built. This added to the already thriving rum-running trade with American anti-prohibitionists.

Flour milling has remained the major industry in the community. A modern mill is now operated by the Robin Hood Flour Company. Other industries that have provided employment and growth to the town include a nickel plant run by Algoma, a shoe manufacturer and a cement plant.

This growth was constant and by 1964 the industry and population of Port Colborne warranted the status of a city.

Today, good harbour facilities cater to pleasure crafts and grain boats. An outdoor farmers' market serves the local people and brings tourists to the downtown area.

PORT DOVER

The first white men to stand on the north shore of Lake Erie at the mouth of Lynn River were French missionaries who lived there for the winter of 1669-70. A little more than a century later an Empire Loyalist by the name of Daniel McQueen arrived at this place and built a mill near the ford of the Lynn River. This site was to become known as Dover Mills and later Port Dover after the English port of Dover.

Dover grew rapidly, thanks to a moderate climate and steamer transport on Lake Erie. During the War of 1812, Port Dover was a supply depot and regular port of call for vessels for the British Navy. In 1814, the Americans, desperate to win the war, burned the settlement to the

The diving horse thrilled the population at Port Dover.

ground. Refusing to admit defeat, the pioneers rebuilt their community and erected new residences closer to the lake.

With the opening of the Welland Canals in 1825-30, the shipping increased on Lake Erie. Merchants of Dover recognized the need to capitalize on this business and petitioned the House of Assembly for permission to improve harbour facilities in 1829. Work began on the harbour in 1833.

Israel Wood Powell owned the land around the harbour. Hoping to witness a new wave of settlers, he laid out a village. A man of vision, he saw his dream fulfilled, particularly by the influx of shipping and fishing industries into the community. The government, in 1842, commenced dredging the harbour and the construction of piers and a lighthouse.

The completion of the Hamilton and Port Dover Plank Road helped to connect with the inland centres of lumber and grain production. Soon Port Dover became a large exporter of grain and lumber. Sawmills were erected throughout the locality to process the lumber that was boomed down the river or drawn in from the forest. From 1850 to 1860, Port Dover's exports of grain and lumber peaked. Warehouses were constructed at the docks and the population rose from 600 to 1,000.

By 1870, the lumber industry had declined and with the construction of railroads inland, Dover began to fail as a major transportation centre. Nine years later the settlers celebrated the incorporation of Port Dover as a village. By this time, despite a tremendous decline of business, Dover was about to awaken to the coming and going of ships again.

The growth of the fishing industry on Lake Erie and the fishermen using Port Dover as a home port brought life back to the dockyards in the 1900's. Plants were erected on the waterfront to proved deep-freeze fish for later processing and distribution to other marketing centres. At one time Port Dover was known for having the largest inland fishing fleet in the world.

Later still many a farmer turned to growing fruit and tobacco, which led to the development of industries to process the harvest. Vacationers discovered the long sandy beaches of Lake Erie and Dover's excellent harbour facilities. Port Dover peaked anew as activities and population were affected by the tourist trade and summer holiday homes.

Dover remains a picturesque town on Lake Erie with hundreds of colourful fishing vessels bobbing up and down in the harbour. Tourists stroll the beach area while snacking on Dover fish fries. The beauty of water and land that attracted the first pioneers to Dover still affects tourists and residents today.

PORT ELGIN

The first white man to settle in the bush that covered the present site of Port Elgin village was Lachlan McLean. It was the fall of 1849 when McLean, after spending a season at the Fishing Islands of Lake Huron, landed at Port Elgin Bay. On land lying just north of Market Street he built a log shanty which was to become a tavern known to all settlers of the Saugeen. George Butchart arrived shortly after McLean and erected a dam and a sawmill across Mill Creek. The name given to the village was in honour of the Earl of ELgin, Governor General at the time.

The presence of a mill and tavern helped to form the nucleus for the village. An early settler by the name of Kennedy described the village at the time in a letter. He wrote, "I was the first storekeeper in the township of Saugeen, having opened a store in what is now the village of Port Elgin on May 27, 1854. At that time the village contained only three houses, a tavern, an unfinished log house that I bought for a store and that had been built by a Mr. Butchart, who had sold out to Benjamin Shantz before I went to Saugeen. I bought the house and one quarter of an acre of land on the corner from Shantz. After opening my store the people got me to petition the Post Office Department to establish a post office. The petition was granted, and I was appointed postmaster. The post office was named Normanton on account of it, at that time, being considered one of the most northern post offices in Canada. The nearest date I can find as to when Normanton P.O. commenced business is about the 16th December, 1854. At that time there was no wagon road through Port Elgin; the mails were brought on foot by a man of the name of John Urquhart, who once a week carried the mail from Kincardine to Southampton."

In 1857, the construction of a pier by private enterprise greatly assisted the arrival of settlers and Port Elgin's export trade. Up until that time when a steamboat entered the bay on its way to Goderich, a large scow had to be rowed out to pick up passengers and freight.

By 1866, Port Elgin had five churches in the village, Methodist, Mennonite, United Brethren, Presbyterian and the Church of the New Jerusalem. It also had two schools, a town hall, four stores, three hotels, a brewery, a woollen factory, a foundry, two sawmills, a grist mill, a pottery, and one physician, Dr. Robert Douglas. The population of the village had risen to 630.

John Hepnor founded the Port Elgin Brush Company in 1883. The factory burned in 1885 but several businessmen rallied behind Mr. Hepnor and raised $20,000 towards rebuilding the factory. In 1896, the business became The Stevens-Hepner Company Limited. In 1908, it bought out a toiletry company, The Dominion Brush Company of Toronto. Another line, Keystone brushes and toilet articles, was added to the existing business of brooms, whisks, and brushes. The company now produces a full range of household and industrial brushes, and imports bristles, wood and other raw materials from several countries around the world. The Stevens-Hepner Company Limited is now the leading industry of Port Elgin.

In recent years Port Elgin has witnessed major change that has been caused by its proximity to the nuclear power station at Douglas Point. Small businesses, employment and land costs reached all-time highs in the 1970's and 80's.

From its humble beginnings with one man residing in a shanty by the shore of Lake Huron, Port Elgin has grown to become a popular summer resort.

PORT STANLEY

The natural harbour of Port Stanley, at the mouth of Kettle Creek on Lake Erie, was so impressive that the early French explorers in the 1600's recorded their observations on sight.

The area remained undisturbed until the nineteenth century when Colonel Thomas Talbot arrived with a grant for two lots on the shores of Lake Erie and Kettle Creek for his friend Colonel John Bostwick. Colonel Bostwick and his family settled here around 1804, and built the first house in Port Stanley. About this time the Minor, Zavitz and Savage families had also taken up residence along the creek. Christian Zavitz and his son Jesse are credited with building a number of mills in the area.

Squire Samuel Price was an interesting character who operated a general store in the village. Part of the time he spent serving customers

An "alligator" boat, so-named because it was used on land and water.

and the rest of the time he administered justice in the courtroom attached to the store.

A rugged road was laid out in 1822 from London to the new settlement. The following year the site was named Port Stanley in honour of Lord Stanley, who was visiting with Colonel Talbot at the time.

In 1827, parliament appointed a commission to investigate the construction of harbour facilities at Port Stanley. The money required was authorized by the government and the construction of the piers began that year. At the time of completion in 1833, the port was already well known on Lake Erie. Imports and exports for the District of London were handled at Port Stanley. By 1843, road conditions were very much improved, and this made stagecoach and wagon-train travel to the village possible. The North American Hotel, established near the east wharf in 1834, was a centre of activity. Stagecoach passengers kept the hotel busy and grain producers required overnight accommodation while waiting for their shipments to be loaded.

In 1844, mariners were delighted to see the installation of a lighthouse on the west pierhead, for better navigation into the harbour. Many people thought Port Stanley ought to have been much larger in order to reflect its immense commercial operations but the population in 1851 remained at six hundred. The small populace was a result of land speculation and high prices for building lots.

When the railway arrived from London in 1856, the shipping industry in Port Stanley declined. Port Stanley remained in this state until the turn of the century, when the potential of three beautiful miles of beachfront on Lake Erie was finally recognized. Suddenly Port Stanley became a fashionable summer resort to be compared to the Burlington Beach Strip, Wasaga Beach, Southampton and Bala, just to mention a few. Society catered, during this period of time, to relaxation, to pleasure and to romanticism.

Today, Port Stanley remains a commercial fishing port and a processing centre. The harbour and the beachfront include marinas and yacht clubs. In the summer the population swells as people come to vacation and relax by the waters of Lake Erie. Many vacationers are a two-hour drive from home. Perhaps Ontario is still the vacation capital of Canada, if not in terms of numbers, certainly in terms of the natural beauty and shimmering waters that were seen here by the French almost four hundred years ago.

QUEENSTON

On the morning of October 13, 1812, the famous Battle of Queenston Heights of the War of 1812 was fought.

Major General Sir Isaac Brock had been busy preparing Upper Canada as well as he could against attack. Trained volunteer soldiers were stationed with the British regulars at posts along the border. Morale was high amongst Canadians, particularly after General Brock had captured Detroit from the Americans during the early days of the war. However, the military remained uneasy about invasion along the Niagara River, between Lake Erie and Lake Ontario, where the American forces numbered seven thousand troops.

After defeating the Americans at Detroit, General Brock quickly left for the Niagara River frontier where only fifteen hundred men stood guard against attack.

On the night of October 12th, General Brock rested at Fort George at the mouth of the Niagara. Just after midnight, the American forces crossed the river at Queenston. Was this the Americans' main attack or a diverson to draw the British force from Fort George? No one was sure. Brock quickly left for Queenston. His second-in-command, General Sheaffe, and the main British force were left behind at Fort George.

The General met a messenger along the road, with news that a great number of the enemy had already crossed the river and more were coming. Brock sent the messenger to Fort George to bring General Sheaffe and his troops along as quickly as possible.

Queenston village was situated at the foot of Queenston Heights, a steep cliff rising some 350 feet from the edge of the Niagara River. The British had strategically placed a gun at the top of the Heights. The Americans came up behind the British gunners by a steep and narrow path. Taken by surprise, the British beat a hasty retreat.

General Brock understood the seriousness of the situation and did not wait for General Sheaffe, but, instead, rallied a small force and charged up the steep hill, sword drawn!

Although he broke the ranks of the American force, he was struck down himself. Suddenly, the British and Canadian lines faltered and retreated to the foot of the hill with their fatally wounded leader.

General Sheaffe had just arrived and took command. He ordered his troops to strike inland. Led by Indian guides, Sheaffe managed a surprise attack on the flank of the Americans. Although the Americans with 1,500 men and another 2,000 waiting to cross the river, heavily out-numbered the opposing force, they panicked and tried to escape. The large force of Americans by the river were ordered to cross, but the troops refused. Many of the enemy retreated by rowing across the river to safety, while others tried to swim and were drowned. The remaining force surrendered to the British and Canadians.

The battle, although victorious, was costly for the British because they lost one of their military leaders, General Isaac Brock. Today a monument stands at Queenston Heights to mark his burial place and to honour the hero of the War of 1812.

Prior to the war, Queenston had on the west bank been settled by United Empire Loyalists and had become the northern terminus of a new portage around Niagara Falls. The old route had been lost when the Americans received the land along the east bank of the river through an agreement between the British and American governments.

Robert Hamilton is considered the founder of Queenston. He owned land here as early as 1789. The name Queenston suggests that it was named for Charlotte, Queen Consort of King George the Third. Others believe the name was derived from the Queen's Rangers, Lieutenant Simcoe's regiment, stationed here in 1792-93. Hamilton was a very ambitous man who built wharves and storehouses and operated a thriving transhipping business. He had been awarded a franchise for a freight carriage business from Queenston to Chippawa. His enterprises were responsible for the riverbank in Queenston becoming a bustling centre of activity and at that time it was named "The Landing". His business ventures were profitable and he built and resided in an impressive stone mansion on the Old River Road. The back rooms overlooked the river. Robert Hamilton raised five children, and one of his sons, George, later became the founder of the city of Hamilton.

During the early nineteenth century Queenston continued to grow. In 1801, the village had become a customs port and one of Upper

A peddlar selling his wares.

Canada's first distributing post offices was established here in 1802. The portage business employed sixty teams of oxen.

The War of 1812 marked the beginning of a slowdown for Queenston. During the war commerce diminished and the economic depression that followed the Napoleonic Wars took its toll. When the Erie Canal opened in 1825 and the Welland in 1829, Queenston's importance as a transportation centre almost ended. Although commercial steamboating on the river kept the port alive, this came to a close in 1855 with the arrival of the Great Western Railway, which linked Toronto to Niagara Falls and other points in America.

Queenston had at one time been the terminus for the first railway in Upper Canada. Chartered in 1835, the Erie and Ontario Railway operated from Queenston to Chippewa over iron-strapped timber rails. The locomotive of the time were unable to pull a train up the steep grade of Queenston Heights. The railway employed trotting horses to draw the passenger coaches and draught horses hauled the freight. The line was eventually extended to Niagara-on-the-Lake.

Attempts were made in later years to revive the freight trade in Queenston. For a time The Niagara Falls Park and River Electric Railway, established in 1893, and the inter-locking steamer-railway service kept commerce alive. The increasing use of motor vehicles in the 1920's heralded the end of these ventures and the population declined as people found work in other centres. When motor transport became convenient and efficient, the peaceful character of Queenston began to attract commuters and by the 1950's the population was on the rise.

This early settlement was also the home of Laura Secord, the famous Canadian heroine who lived here during the War of 1812. It was from Queenston that she set out on an arduous journey to warn James Fitzgibbon of an impending American invasion. Her home has been restored and is now open to the public. Another former resident was Reformer William Lyon Mackenzie, who published the Colonial Advocate here in 1824. His residence and printing shop have been restored and visitors are also welcome there.

Today Queenston is a residential community with its heritage prominently displayed. The main source of revenue is tourism.

SAINTE-MARIE-AMONG-THE-HURONS

An aerial view of Sainte-Marie-among-the-Hurons.

The town of Midland, located in the heart of historic Huronia, was once populated by the Huron Nation. Near the site of the present town, French Jesuit Missionaries established a mission called Sainte-Marie-among-the-Hurons in 1639. Sainte-Marie, at that time, was the most westerly outpost of white civilization. This fortified centre was a place of refuge for the Huron Indian converts and the site of Ontario's first church and hospital.

The story of Sainte-Marie begins with the arrival of Samuel de Champlain who, in 1608, established a settlement at Quebec. The new land was called New France after Jacques Cartier had claimed it for France in 1534. From 1535 to 1540, New France grew slowly into a colony.

By 1634, Trois Rivieres was established, then Sillery, near Quebec, and Sainte-Marie in 1639, and finally Ville Marie, Montreal, in 1642. At that time, New France was run by a trading company in France.

The Society of Jesus (Jesuits) was formed in 1534 by Ignatius Loyola. During the 17th century the Society became a world-wide missionary and teaching branch of the Roman Catholic Church.

The first Jesuits arrived in Huronia in 1626. Huronia stretched from north-west of Lake Simcoe to the south-east of Georgian Bay, covering 340 square miles. Their confederation consisted of four tribes bearing the names of Cord, Rock, Deer and Bear. In 1618, Champlain put the population at 30,000, inhabiting twenty villages. The Hurons built their villages close to a good water supply and arable soil, surrounded by natural defence features. They lived in longhouses measuring twenty to thirty feet wide, similar in height and eighty to one hundred feet long. The villages moved to a new site every twenty to forty years.

In 1634, Champlain proposed that the French and the Hurons become one Catholic people. Between 1634 and 1640, the Hurons came under increasing exposure to Western Christian ideals. Contact with the Jesuits introduced many fatal diseases to the Hurons. Smallpox, measles and influenza ravaged the native population. In 1639, the Jesuits did a lodge to lodge count and discovered that only 12,000 natives remained alive. It was between 1640 and 1650 that the Hurons took charge of the fur trade with the French.

The alliance with the Hurons presented other advantages for the French. By allying themselves with the Hurons the French were committing themselves to lend military support against the Iroquois, their hereditary enemies.

Meanwhile, the Iroquois aspired to have the same relationship with the Dutch the Hurons had with the French. Furs began to be scarce in the Iroquois territory, south of Huronia, and the Iroquois plotted to exterminate the Hurons and gain control of the fur trade. This was supported by the Dutch who were aware that the ruin of the Huron meant the end of the French trade and of New France.

On September 7, 1644, Father Jean de Brébeuf, a Jesuit missionary who had lived and worked among the Hurons was sent back to Huronia by his superiors. This was at the precise moment when the death struggle of the Huron nation was beginning. By 1647, the Iroquois were attacking in the heart of Huron Country. Suddenly Jesuit missions became easy targets for the Iroquois. On March 15, 1649, a war party of some 1,200 well-armed Iroquois arrived completely undetected at the frontier of

One of the many longhouses at Sainte-Marie-among-the-Hurons.

Huronia. They approached the village of Saint Ignace during the night of March 15th, and attacked at day break. Once a breach was made in the palisade they quickly over-ran the village while the inhabitants were asleep.

In a short time four hundred Hurons were killed with only a loss of ten Iroquois. Three Huron men managed to escape and travelled to Sainte-Louis, a village just a league away. Father Brébeuf and Father Gabriel Lalemant were at Sainte-Louis, on a visit from Sainte-Marie.

As soon as word of the capture of Sainte-Ignace reached Sainte-Louis, five hundred women and children fled the village at once, while the men prepared to face the enemy. The Hurons numbered eighty, a pitifully small force to meet the Iroquois onslaught. Many begged the two Fathers to escape while they could, but ther zeal did not permit them. The salvation of their flock was dearer to them than love for their own lives.

A force of 1,000 Iroquois arrived at the village before sunrise and launched an attack. The Hurons repelled the first assault, and then a second; but on the third assault the Iroquois broke through the palisade of stakes and captured the village.

At nine o'clock that morning smoke from the burning cabins at Sainte-Louis caught the attention of those at Sainte-Marie, just a league distant. Two Huron Indians who had escaped reached Sainte-Marie with the news of the capture and seizure of Brébeuf and Lalement. The two fathers were then dragged off to Sainte-Ignace (halfway between Cold-water and Vasey in the County of Simcoe). Meanwhile, the Iroquois decided to attack Sainte-Marie on the following morning.

At Sainte-Marie the French readied themselves for the battle to come. Huron warriors, mostly from La Conception, on hearing the news of the Iroquois attacks, assembled quickly in front of Sainte-Marie and set themselves in ambush. When the vanguard of the Iroquois, about two hundred strong, moved against Sainte-Marie the next morning, they were intercepted by the Hurons. After a violent encounter, the Iroquois were chased back to the smouldering remains of Sainte-Louis. The main body of the Iroquois army quickly came to the aid of their brethren. A fierce battle ensued in which the Hurons were defeated but not before slaying one hundred Iroquois and seriously wounding an Iroquois chief. Discouraged by the loss of their warriors, and alarmed at the rumours of a large Huron force on the way, the Iroquois withdrew from Huronia.

The fate of Brébeuf and Lalemant was soon discovered. At the time of their capture they were stripped of flesh to the very bone. The Iroquois poured boiling water over several parts of Brébeuf's body in mockery of Holy Baptism. A collar of hot hatchets was then placed on his shoulders and stomach. His lips were cut off after he constantly spoke of God. His body received over two hundred blows from a club. His eyes were gouged with burning coals and yet he managed to live through three hours of such torture. As an act of respect for his courage and to acquire some themselves, the Iroquois cut out his heart and ate it. Father Lalement endured fifteen hours of the same torture before he died. Both men were later buried at Sainte-Marie.

In the weeks that followed, thousands of Hurons were in need of care at Sainte-Marie and within two months the missionaries destroyed and abandoned Sainte-Marie and retreated with the Hurons to Christian Island on Georgian Bay.

On June 21, 1925, the eight martyrs of New France, who had met with fates similiar to Brébeuf and Lalement, were beatified by the Pope. On June 26, 1926, the Martyrs Shrine was built near Sainte-Marie to honour the martyrs.

In 1941, the Society of Jesus and the Royal Ontario Museum began an archeological dig in the area under the direction of Kenneth Kidd. In 1954, Father Hagerty of the Society of Jesus found the graves of Father Brébeuf and Father Lalement.

In 1967, as a centennial project, Sainte-Marie-among-the-Hurons was accurately reconstructed and opened to the public. Today the authentic reconstruction of the mission is complemented by guided tours, historical interpreters, and a museum. On the site, the emphasis is on understanding the realities of a mission in the wilderness in the seventeenth century and on honouring the courage and faith of the Jesuits and Hurons alike.

SARNIA

Once it was a fur trading post named The Rapids; now it is the city of Sarnia and its origins go back to the arrival of Ignace Cazelet in 1807. In those days this settlement by the St. Clair River consisted of a few log shanties owned by a handful of French settlers and traders. The land was Chippewa hunting territory governed by Chief Puckinans and later by his son, Chief Wawanosh. The French leased their land from the Chippewa until 1827, when they surrendered their lands in exchange for a reserve.

Jean Baptiste first settled here in 1808 and built on the site where the public library now stands. Shortly thereafter, Father Fluette established himself here and ministered to the Roman Catholics along the river.

One of the first English-speaking settlers was Lieutenant Richard E. Vidal in 1832. The Lieutenant had been interested in the possibilities of seaway traffic since 1816, during his first visit to The Rapids while in the service. He immediately initiated a trade route from this point on the St. Clair River to Detroit.

Although he was a daring and enterprising young man, he learned quickly that he was not the only settler who was innovative. During one of his periodic visits to England, Lieutenant Vidal's home on Front Street was occupied by the Ferguson family of eight. The Fergusons perceived a need for a tavern in the settlement, and consequently they adapted the

Sarnia waterfront scene in 1873.

Vidal home for such purposes during his absence. Upon his return the Lieutenant discovered the changes to his property and evicted them without ceremony.

Sarnia was named to honour the Governor of Canada who was appointed in 1828, Sir John Colborne. At one time he had served as Governor of the Channel Island of Guernsey for which the Roman name was Sarnia. Governor Colborne was the founder of Upper Canada College.

Sir John arrived at The Rapids in 1835 and at the time a dispute was underway about renaming the community. The English favoured "Buenos Aires" and the Scots wanted the name to be "New Glasgow". To break the deadlock, Sir John suggested the name Port Sarnia and the community agreed to accept it.

Port Sarnia had its fair share of influential settlers. There was George Durand, who operated a small store and became the first postmaster in 1837 and Malcolm Cameron, who established himself, about the same time, in the lumbering business and eventually expanded into building and operating ships out of Port Sarnia's natural harbour. He had lived previously in Lanark County, where he had served as a

Chinese immigrants entering Sarnia via the Sarnia Tunnel Railway, c. 1900.

member of Parliament. Through his efforts, a road was built from Sarnia to London.

When the population exceeded 800 in 1856, Sarnia was incorporated as a town and appointed county town. The Great Western Railway was in operation by then and helped to determine its importance as a trade centre. The discovery of oil and the subsequent establishment of a refinery, in 1871, assisted greatly in the growth of the settlment. Between 1880 and 1907, more than 150 oil wells came into operation. Salt was another product discovered in the area, and is, today, one of Sarnia's oldest industries.

In 1890, Sarnia was linked up to Port Huron, Michigan, by a tunnel beneath the St. Clair River. When it was completed in 1891, this 6,026 foot tunnel was considered to be one of the finest engineering feats in the world. The Grand Trunk Railway received great benefit from speedy access to the American side of the river.

On May 7, 1914, Sarnia became a city. People foresaw the incredible growth of the petro-chemical industry that did eventually concentrate here. The products now under manufacture include, urethane foam, Tolvene Di-isocyanate, oil furnace carbon black for use in the rubber industry, anhydrous ammonia, dry and liquid fertilizer materials,

Liquid Petroleum gas, styrene, and a host of chemical, plastic and pharmaceutical items. Dow Chemical, operating here since the 1940's now puts out more than 700 chemical materials.

From 1972 to 1978 a billion dollars was spent on new and expanded plants, which employed 7,000 construction workers. From 1982 to 1984 further plant expansions costing another billion were carried out by 4,000 workers.

Each year the industries of Sarnia contribute upwards of 10 million dollars to the city tax collections. About twenty industries employ more than 10,000 people and Imperial Oil alone pays more than 100 million a year in salaries.

In 1977, Sarnia became the first recipient of a 1.1 million loan under the Ontario Downtown Revitalization Program. This loan and others brought the overall expenditures for re-vitalization of the downtown core up to more than 5.5 million dollars. At the same time almost 20 million was spent on various construction projects within the downtown core.

The history of Sarnia seems always to have been rooted in the soil. The native people and fur trappers obtained their sustenance from the surface of the land, while later settlers sought what was below the surface. Pollution of the air and water is now of major concern so where will future generations look for new endeavours?

SAUBLE BEACH

Near Stoney Point on South Sauble Beach there is an ancient Indian burial ground. Here there is one grave, specially marked, of a white woman. Stolen from her home in Niagara Peninsula when she was a small child, she was raised by the native people to become the wife of their future chief. When she was finally traced by her parents, whose frantic search had never ceased, this loyal wife and mother refused to leave her family and new home. She had known only love and kindness from her captors and chose to remain a part of that culture. She and her chosen family still share space in the little cemetery within the sound of the waves of Lake Huron.

Workmen taking a break at Sauble Falls.

South and North Sauble Beach, Sauble Falls and Chief's Point Indian reserve were once the scene of many fierce battles. The reserve owes its name to the fact that this was once the meeting place of tribal chiefs. On October 13th, 1854, the native people relinquished all other land on the Saugeen Peninsula. "Confiding in the wisdom and protecting care of our Great Mother across the Big Lake. . ." (Queen Victoria), fourteen members of Indian tribes signed along with Lawrence Oliphant, Superintendent General for Indian Affairs. In payment for this land, which included the Township of Amabel, a sum of money was set aside, the interest on which (known as treaty money) was to be paid twice yearly to the people 'as long as grass grows and water runs'.

The first major centre of activity was Sauble Falls. This thriving little hamlet, started in 1869, once had a post office, a blacksmith shop, a boarding house, a store and a large sawmill. A sawmill was erected by R. Head on a land grant issued in 1869 to John McKenzie. In 1937 the mill was destroyed by fire. At one time, Sauble Beach sported a creamery and cheese factory.

In its early days, North Sauble Beach was a fishermen's paradise. The Vary family who lived here kept large cages anchored in the Sauble River to hold their catch of Sturgeon. The Mothersell family and several native families from Chief's Point Reserve also made their living from fishing. Fresh water herring were so plentiful that they were hauled away by the wagon load. Hepworth Store keepers bartered goods for fish and Johnson's cooper shop was busy building barrels in order to ship fish greater distances.

Among the first people to camp on this crescent-shaped sandy beach, that stretched eleven kilometres along Lake Huron, were the Cordingly and Lawson families. In 1905, the Eldridge family built the first summer cottage and in the spring of 1906, the Cordingly cottage went up. Among the names of families once prominent in community life at Sauble Beach and Sauble Falls, are Althouse, Atchison, Adamson, Byers, Clifford, Dawns, Holmes, Johnson, Nicholson, Walker and many more.

Cottages quickly spread and in no time at all three post offices – North Sauble, Sauble Beach and South Sauble – were required to handle the mail. An active business section was constructed at the main entrance to the beach and by the late 1960's the Scott-Robertson Enterprises operated the Beach Pavilion, The Gift Bowl, The Roller Rink and hosted movies once a week. There is also a nine-hole golf course, a go-cart track, kiddieland and a midway.

The name Sauble Beach is known widely in Ontario. It is a favourite summer resort and plays a significant role in Amabel Township as an attraction to motorists and a source of revenue.

Today summer residences number in the thousands and numerous hotels along the shallow beach of Lake Huron, to the north and to the south, bring a different kind of activity to the area. Gone is the lumber industry and the commercial fishing business. In its place is a tourism industry that proves to be profitable enough to continue each year.

Tourists find it hard to leave this picturesque spot that offers so much and perhaps they understand another reason why the fair-skinned woman chose not leave but to listen eternally to the lapping waves of Lake Huron.

SIMCOE

A Sunday afternoon picnic in Simcoe.

The town of Simcoe traces its early beginning to a visit by Sir John Graves Simcoe in 1795. He stopped here overnight on his way to establish Fort Norfolk on Lake Erie and later he granted lands in the area to potential settlers.

Aaron Culver was among the first colonizers to receive land on the condition that he build mills. An ambitious man, he set about constructing a sawmill and a grist mill on the bank of Lynn River. Before long, like many Ontario communities, a settlement had grown around them.

During the War of 1812, the invading Americans torched his mills and looted several houses but the Simcoe settlers were determined to stay, and they repaired the damage and continued on with their lives. In 1815, a Captain Bird arrived and purchased land from Aaron Culver. In short order Captain Bird attained the status of a prominent merchant in the settlement. He was honoured when the citizens called their hamlet Birdtown.

Between 1819 and 1823, Culver divided his property into village lots and proposed that the village be named Simcoe in remembrance of the late Lieutenant-Governor. Several businessmen, who were located in the north end of the community, opposed the name. They favoured the name of Wellington. Simcoe became the official name, but the name of Wellington remained the name for the north end of the town. To this day the name Wellington is commemorated in a park in Simcoe.

The Simcoe post office opened in 1829, and a courthouse and gaol were constructed in 1836. By 1851, Simcoe was incorporated as a village.

The early industries in the village included Peachey and Sons, a foundry that designed and built the "alligator tug", a tugboat that was capable not only of operating on water but also on land by use of cables and winches. The alligator tugs greatly assisted in the operations of the bustling lumber industry. The arrival of the railroad in 1872 linked Simcoe to Fort Erie. Three years later a line was connected from Woodstock to Port Dover via Simcoe. This line greatly increased the population of Simcoe and it was incorporated as a town in 1878.

Simcoe experienced a new type of growth and prosperity during the 1920's. The flue-cured tobacco industry began in the area and farmers turned to fruit growing, a valuable cash crop. Processing plants were built which drew more people to the area and a large tin can manufacturing plant established in the 1930's gave employment opportunities a boost. Tobacco and fruit products still form the nucleaus of the industrial sector.

Maple-lined streets and an elegant park complimented by Victorian homes make Simcoe a model Ontario town. The Eva Brook- Donley Museum, housed in a restored mansion, exhibits a varied collection, from paintings to microfilm, from native artifacts to Victorian furniture. The cultural appetite of the residents of Simcoe is satisfied by the Lynnwood Arts Centre. This impressive gallery features exhibits of sculpture, drawings, painting and stained glass by noted artists.

Simcoe still reflects the charming Victorian era of Ontario. Situated twenty-four miles south of Brantford, Simcoe reminds one of a town in the Old South, surrounded by fields of lush vegetation, large, old trees, massive homes and winding rivers. Even the pace of life seems slower.

SOUTHAMPTON

A sunny afternoon at Southampton Beach.

The early history of the Southampton area and of the Saugeen River goes back to a time before the arrival of settlers when the Ojibways and Iroquois feuded over trading territory.

The two nations allowed one another peaceful trading trips to Montreal until bands of Iroquois waylaid several returning parties of Ojibways all at once. It was the fall of the year and already too late in the season to commence warlike operations; retaliation was put off until the following spring and allies were contacted. In the month of the following May, combined forces gathered in two parties, one at Lake St. Clair, the other at Sault Ste. Marie. Seven hundred canoes were assembled at the Sault and divided into two bands. One advanced on the Iroquois by way of the Ottawa Valley; one proceeded to Penetanguishene and at the same time, the Lake St. Clair division came up the east coast of Lake Huron to the mouth of the Saugeen River. A fierce battle ensued. The Iroquois fled before the onslaught of the Ojibways. The Ojibways retained possession of these territories until they were surrendered by treaty to the Crown on August 9, 1836.

The first settlement at Southampton was made by Captains John Spence and William Kennedy. Both men had been in the employ of the Hudson's Bay Company, and had retired in 1847 to take up residence at Kingston. Having heard of the profitablility of the Lake Huron Fisheries, they decided to investigate for themselves and travelled to Lake Simcoe. They purchased a canoe at Rama from the Indians and proceeded to the mouth of the Saugeen via the Severn River and Georgian Bay.

They arrived in June of 1848 and by winter they had erected a log house. Captain Kennedy remained until 1852, when, at the request of Lady Franklin, he went in search of Sir John Franklin who was lost with the expedition to find the Northwest Passage.

By 1857, 130 houses marked the size of the village. The business portion of the settlement was north of High Street, on Huron and Grosvenor Streets. There were six shops, two hotels and five warehouses. A planing mill stood on the beach near a mineral water spring and a steam sawmill sat on the river's edge.

In 1870-71 contracts were let for the construction of a harbour, starting with a pier from Chantry Island towards the shore, and one from the shore outwards. This created a protected entrance to the harbour. A lighthouse erected in 1859 at Chantry Island was 94 feet above high water and sent its guiding rays out over a fifteen-mile radius. The fishing

A view of the Southampton River dock.

industry of Southampton had seventy men manning eighteen boats in 1855, and a capital investment of $30,000.

Fire struck the village early in the morning of November 4, 1886 and within four hours everything for two blocks along High Street was burned to the ground. More than fifty buildings were consumed and thirty families left homeless with total losses amounting to $60,000.

In 1904, Southampton was eligible for town status and A.E. Belcher was elected mayor for 1905. The population has not increased greatly in this century. A tannery, a mineral bottling works, a sawmill and the shipping docks contributed to employment at the turn of the century. Later industries included furniture factories, among which Knechtel was dominant for years. Solomon Knechtel came to Southampton in 1895 as manager of the Knechtel Furniture Company, where the Hepworth Furniture Company stands today.

For many years, Peter Knechtel operated the Chippawa Lumber Company near the mouth of the river. It was a sawmill and a planing mill. The mill was taken over by Diebel and Eldridge who purchased logs from the Indians but dwindling sources closed the mill.

In 1906 the signs of decline in the fishing industry were visible. The arrival in great numbers of the lamprey eel and of smelts proved to be disastrous for commercial fishermen. The catches of lake trout fell noticeably. It was not until 1946, that the Canadian and American governments opted to work on the eel problem.

By 1955, no lake trout were to be found and the commercial fishing industry was finished. The decline of fishing saw the growth of tourism and in the last forty years Southampton has become a busy resort area. The Breakers Hotel, Hampton Court, the Walker House, several hotels and some private homes provide accommodation for hundreds of tourists. The wide main street with speciality shops and dining facilities cater to this change in economic base. The museum hosts numerous exhibitions and also displays the complete history of the area. It is one of the finest historical museums in Ontario.

Southampton has miles of excellent beach area on which you can wander the Huron shoreline and stand in awe of magnificent sunsets.

STRATFORD

A survey party, sent out by the Canada Company in 1828, tramped through the wilds of the Huron Tract until they came to a bend where the road crossed a stream. Here they paused and crude shelters were erected for convenience. A few months down the road, Colonel Anthony Van Egmond of the Canada Company purchased the land by the river crossing.

The Canada Company expropriated Van Egmond's lands for a townsite in 1832. A street plan was laid out and the company supervised the building of a millpond and grist mill. A hotel, constructed and operated on the south bank by William Sargeant and his wife, was titled Shakespeare Inn. The picturesque setting of the new settlement inspired an official to donate a painting of the bard to the inn. Sometime later the community was named Stratford and the stream was called the Avon, after Stratford-upon-Avon in England. The Sargeant's Inn served as an inn and tavern to travellers and settlers of the area and also as a church on Sunday.

In 1834, George Worsley opened a store in one of the abandoned shanties on the north shore. A post office followed shortly thereafter and the business area began to expand.

With the Municipal Act of 1850, Perth County separated from Bruce and Huron Counties, and the tiny settlement of Stratford, on the Avon River, was chosen as the county seat of Perth. Two years later the county buildings were erected in the village.

Two railway lines arrived in 1856, and Stratford became a junction centre. Expansion of the village coincided with the railway and the new employment it provided for the community. A triangular town centre was developed on Downie Street between the river and the two south-end station sites. An impressive town hall and several market buildings were completed by 1857. A year later town status became a reality.

The year 1871 marked real economic beginnings for Stratford when a railway engine shop was built. This new industry offered employment to hundreds of families new to the area. A thriving grain export business added to the development of commerce.

For eighty years rail services provided the majority of the employment in Stratford. When diesel engines replaced steam engines and when

Stratford ceased to be a junction centre in the 1950's, 2000 jobs disappeared. These jobs have been replaced by new industries.

There are now thirty-two manufacturing firms in Stratford that employ twenty-five or more people each and eleven companies with one hundred or more employees each. Civic policy has done a beautiful job of keeping industry away from the parkland and the downtown area of Stratford.

By 1953, the citizens of Stratford felt the need to expand culturally. During that year Thomas Patterson of Stratford came up with the idea of a Shakespearean Festival. The event first originated in a tent theatre, in the park by the Avon River, and that first season, Sir Alec Guinness played the lead in 'Richard the Third'.

In 1957 the tent theatre was replaced by the Festival theatre, a building designed by Canadian architect Robert Fairfield to be built at a cost of over two million dollars. The stage of the main theatre, designed by Tanja Moisciwitsch in conjunction with British director Tyrone Guthrie, was revolutionary for its time. Guthrie wanted a return to the open stage of the Elizabethans, but not an antiquarian replica. The ampitheatre is steeply sloped, with a 220-degree sweep around the stage. Although the auditorium seats 2,262 on three sides of the stage, no spectator is further than 19.8 metres from the stage.

The festival later acquired two additional stages. The Avon Theatre, seating capacity 1,102, in downtown Stratford was purchased in 1963 and subsequently redesigned by Moiseiwitsch. It has a conventional proscenium stage. Since 1971 the festival has also presented drama and music at a Third Stage, a small, modestly-equipped theatre suitable for workshops, experimental presentations and the training of young actors. The annual Stratford festival continues to play to thousands of tourists.

Where wooden shanties once stood beside the river, white swans nest. If the Canada Company could see the growth of the natural beauty they surveyed so long ago they would be justifiably proud.

St. Catharines

Rodman Hall, the home of William H. Merritt as it appeared c. 1905.

St. Catharines, prior to the arrival of the white man, was the most heavily populated native settlement in North America. The burial grounds alone covered an area of five or six acres.

Now known as the Garden City of Canada for its display of blossoms, St. Catharines' recorded history began when John Hainer and Jacob Dittrick arrived here in 1790. Both men were United Empire Loyalists and they settled across the creek from one another. Two years later Thomas Adams arrived and opened a tavern at Twelve Mile Creek. An enterprising man, Adams soon owned and operated a sawmill and a grist mill. Paul Shipman later took over the tavern.

Many of the early settlers were disbanded soldiers who had fought with "Butler's Rangers" during the Revolutionary War. In a short space of time, the community of St. Catharines numbered fifty settlers, who named the place to honour the first wife of the Honourable Robert Hamilton, Superintendent of the Western District. Catharine Hamilton had died in 1796. Previously, the community was called "The Twelve" or "Shipman's Corners".

The story of St. Catharines would not be complete without the story of William Merritt.

William Merritt first entered into the business world at age sixteen, when he went into partnership with a Mr. Chisholm in a general store. By age nineteen he had sold his interest in the business and returned to work on the family homestead. He found that the outdoor work helped his health, his spirits and his creativity.

With the advent of the War of 1812, Merritt joined to fight for his country and quickly rose to Captain of the Provincial, or Niagara Dragoons and fought throughout Southern Ontario. Shortly after the proclamation of peace, he lost no time in exchanging the bonds of war for those of matrimony, with Catharine Prendergest of Mayville, New York.

Mr. Merritt, upon realizing that the war had effected great material shortages in the country, purchased twenty-five acres of land at Shipman's Corners for $625. There he built a large house, half of which he used for his home and the remainder for a general store. Later it was converted into a hotel, and eventually burned down.

A few salt springs were found in Upper Canada. One of these salt springs was on the Merritt property on the Twelve. In addition to his

A ladies military regiment standing in front of the courthouse, c. 1890's.

other undertakings, he had the spring cleaned up and properly curbed, and in August, 1816, he began to manufacture salt. St. Catharines gained a reputation as a health resort with its salt and mineral springs and Dr. William Chase was the first to promote medicinal use of the springs.

The idea of a waterway that would connect Lakes Erie and Ontario was first proposed in a bill to the Legislative Assembly of Upper Canada in 1799. The bill was brought up again in 1816, but was defeated. Within two years William Hamilton Merritt took up the cause and eventually saw it to its completion. This idea became the achievement of his lifetime.

Merritt first got the idea after rebuilding a grist mill on the Twelve. He quickly discovered that the water supply for his mill was too limited in the summer months. He conceived the notion of obtaining a further supply from the Chippewa River, the summit of which was two miles distant. He concluded, with friends George Keefer and John DeCew, that a canal could be dug to connect Lake Ontario to the Welland River by using the valley of the Twelve Mile Creek. The men presented a petition in 1818 to the legislature to make a proper survey for a canal over this route. The authorities favoured a canal further west, between the Grand River and Hamilton. Five years later in March of 1823, Merritt persuaded a group of people to support the survey of his route by a competent engineer. Encouraged by the engineer's report, Merritt and local residents were granted incorporation of the Welland Canal Company on January 19, 1824, by an act of legislature.

On the 30th of the same month, the turning of the first sod took place at present-day Allanburg. Disappointed by the turn-out Merritt quickly stated, "We have determined to depend on others no longer, but to apply our own shoulders to the wheel and set about it in good earnest." What began as a passage for small canal boats ended as a waterway for lake vessels. The canal on the Twelve was completed by May of 1828.

The construction of the Welland Canal was quite an achievement considering the methods employed and the tools of the day. No excavating machinery existed and all power was supplied by men, horses, and oxen. The canal measured twenty-eight miles long with a depth throughout of eight feet. A writer by the name of Ernest Green later wrote, "The development of the Niagara Peninsula in the two decades following the commencement of the Welland Canal was at such a rate as is usually associated only with the discovery of gold fields or diamond mines."

A deserted red building on Brewery Street at the foot of Oak Hill Park in St. Catharines, is all that remains of the Taylor and Bate Brewery built in 1834. The original Stagecoach Inn was once located on Pelham Road north, at a place called "Hangmans's Corner". It is said that during the War of 1812, several captured Americans were hanged here.

Shipbuilding became a large industry in St. Catharines, with the famous Shickluna yard that employed hundreds of men. Lewis Shickluna, a native of Malta came to St. Catharines in 1836. He located his shipbuilding yard below where the Burgoyne Bridge now spans the ravine. Over one hundred and twenty steamers were launched from this yard.

The village of St. Catharines was incorporated as a town in 1845. The Welland House, one of many hotels, was built in 1853 by a number of emancipated negro slaves who escaped from the United States to Canada. The Zion Baptist Church on 82 Geneva Street was built by the same workers on 1863.

On May 1, 1876, flags fluttered from the tops of most downtown buildings to mark St. Catharines first day as a city. There was much to celebrate. The Welland Canal had greatly assisted in the industrialization of St. Catharines. The creation of mills, shipyards and metal fabrication plants had brought great prosperity. The Great Western Railway in 1859 linked St. Catharines to other Ontario centres. Manufacturing evolved from domestic goods and the carriage trade to automobile production and accessories, wineries, canning factories and paper companies.

The wine industry began in 1873 when George Barnes opened a large winery that is still operating today. A year later, Thomas Bright founded Bright's Wines, Canada's largest winery.

Development progressed steadily in the 20th century. The Lincoln Historical Society was founded in 1927 to preserve the country's early history and a War Memorial was unveiled that same year by Edward, Prince of Wales, in Memorial Park.

Manufacturing in St. Catharines in 1978 included 135 establishments with 15,759 employees. Four establishments in St. Catharines employ two-thirds of the labour force and, of these, General Motors is the largest.

Effective January 1, 1961 the former towns of Merritton and Port Dalhousie and the major portion of the township of Grantham amalgamated with St. Catharines swelling the city's population to over 90,000.

The city has its own symphony orchestra, a municipal airport, a famous annual regatta, a long-established daily newspaper, The Standard, and the well-known Rodman Hall Art Gallery.

ST. JACOBS

The hardware store at St. Jacobs.

Jacob C. Snider, a Mennonite farmer and pioneer industrialist, never stopped dreaming of carving new business ideas out of an old undisturbed forest. At the end of the War of 1812, he arrived in Canada and embarked on his career in the village of Waterloo where he became well known for his many commercial endeavours.

As early as 1830, Jacob and John B. Baumann, whose house overlooked the wooden bridge of the Conestoga River, discussed the possibilities of a mill for a village.

The first step that Snider took to help realize this dream was to purchase one acre of Lot 36 and 162 acres of Lot 8 from John Baumann. Jacob bought four acres of Lot 7 from Simon Cress in 1849 and quickly negotiated with farmers up the river for long-term leases of land that might be flooded by a new dam near the Arthur Road. The three-foot dam was completed in 1851, and provided water power for a sawmill and a woollen mill. A flour mill was soon under construction and was operational in 1852. The mills formed the nucleus of a growing settlement. To ensure further impetus, Snider, John Buamann and Ephraim Kress had lots surveyed and sold them to incoming settlers. Snider also had a blacksmith shop in operation by this time.

Jacob C. Snider and his son of the same name were instrumental in establishing this new settlement, but others took advantage of the opportunity to share in the new economic possibilities. Two gentlemen, by the names of Bemus and Chalmers, opened a general store and a store was opened by George W. Eby, a grandson of the first Mennonite settler in the township. Gregory Hortenberger opened the first cooper shop which was also the first brick building. Cooperage, the construction of barrels, was among the earliest industries in the hamlet.

Local farmers who watched the settlement by the river grow, referred to it as Jakobstettel or "Jacobs" village. In 1852, when a post office opened the residents chose the name St. Jacobs.

Early industries in the village included the tannery of Hopkins and Buck, and Jacob Eby's large frame furniture factory. John George and F.W. Welz were carriage makers and John Ruehl and Sons were furniture manufacturers.

Eventually St. Jacobs had four hotels operating in the village. The Snider family owned a distillery located a short distance upstream from the flour mill. The St. Jacobs Distillery was capable of producing 40 to 80 gallons of spirits per day, more than enough to satisfy the thirst of the settlers of Woolwich Township.

Mennonite views on the subject of drinking were quite tolerant at first, but in 1842 and again in 1844, a General Conference was held to discuss the effects of excessive drinking on the settlement. Some people were in favour of total abstinence, but the stand adopted only came out against the manufacture of hard liquor. Even at that, the medicinal properties were acknowledged.

Eventually, the various industries of the village attracted newcomers who were not Mennonites. Although they picked up the dialect and in many ways the mannerisms of their Mennonite neighbours, few adopted the Mennonite beliefs. On the other hand, the Mennonites of the district were so self-sufficient that they required little of the services available in St. Jacobs.

Jacob Snider's mill was eventually taken over by his son, Elias Weaver Bigman Snider. This new owner introduced European techniques to flour milling and by 1875, he installed the first roller flour milling system in the country. This new, fine flour was sold throughout Canada and the eastern United States.

The image of St. Jacobs today differs considerably from yesteryear and yet has preserved the flavour. The industry of the community primarily caters to tourists rather than the locals. Occasionally, a Mennonite with a horse and buggy is seen on the main street like a flashback in time. St. Jacobs is situated on the main highway and the Mennonite buggies have no choice but to mingle with the traffic. The village is so busy during the summer months that this poses great difficulty for these people.

On either side of the street in this small settlement, there are period-style shops of every possible description. The old mill on the main street by the river has been converted into multiple-level shopping for a wide range of artisans. Production and sales are combined and tourists can watch these people make everything that is sold – art, jewellery, clothing, toys and more. The blacksmith shop, still in regular operation, is a popular stop for most people visiting the village. The Meeting Place Museum houses the fascinating history of the Mennonite community, portrayed by displays and audio visuals.

For most towns history is the recorded past, but for St. Jacobs it is visible in the living present.

ST. THOMAS

During the early days of settlement, the government of Upper Canada encouraged immigration by granting and selling land to those men who promised to promote it as well. One man who took the government up on their offer and who later became the most famous promoter of colonization in Upper Canada was Colonel Thomas Talbot.

Talbot started out with a land grant of 5,000 acres on the north shore of Lake Erie. The government allowed him 200 acres of land for each settler that he placed on fifty acres. Talbot made his own rules and acted like a dictator over these colonists. Applicants for land were required to meet with the Colonel at his home. When they arrived, he would discuss business through the open window. Once he had granted a settler a piece of land, their name was written in pencil on a plan. If a settler neglected his duties or displeased Talbot, his name was erased.

His success lay in the roads that connected the backwoods farms to the settlements. He was instrumental in formulating an ingenious set of rules to be adhered to by settlers. The first rule required any settler to clear half the road in front of their lot, and to keep it open all year. Eventually, this became a county road that was linked with the settlement. A settler had to clear ten acres of their farm and build a house. After five years of fulfilling his duties and of remaining on the land, Talbot would issue such a settler a certificate that could be exchanged for a legal title.

Rumour had it that Talbot was a lonely man who lived in a simple log home, a man who had a mark on the wall and would start drinking once the rays of the sun rested upon that mark.

The capital of the Talbot settlement was St. Thomas, named after the Colonel with the Saint prefixed merely as a euphemism. Formerly known as Kettle Creek, the village was situated on Kettle Creek about sixteen miles south of London. The first families to settle here in 1810, were Captain R.D. Drake, Garret Smith, Captain Daniel Rapelje, Archibald McNeland and Mr. Curtis.

Daniel Rapelje settled on 200 acres on the south side of the Talbot Road at Kettle Creek. A veteren of the War of 1812 and Captain of the 1st Middlesex Militia, Rapelje returned in 1814 and began construction of a grist mill on his property. The war along the Lake Erie shore had left only two mills operating in the region. The potential for further settlement inspired him to lay out part of his farm into village lots and then sell them to newcomers. Because he was a man of religious principles, he donated the land for the St. Thomas Anglican church and cemetery. It was Colonel Talbot who donated the necessary funds for the construction of a tower, a steeple and the chancel for the church. The church still stands today and is a fine example of the early English Gothic Revival style.

Part of the Elgin County Pioneer Museum is housed in the original homestead of Dr. Elijah Duncombe, built in 1848. His brother, Dr. Charles Duncombe, settled on the same property during the 1820's. He and Dr. John Rolph opened in 1824 the first medical school in Upper Canada. It was called the Talbot Dispensatory. Charles Duncombe was an active supporter of the William Lyon Mackenzie Reform Party and took an active part in the Rebellion of 1837. This involvement forced him to flee to the United States.

St. Thomas was incorporated as a village in 1853. A year later the first substantial brick buildings were started on Talbot Street. Fire struck on Christmas morning of 1870 and destroyed most of the business section of the village. St. Thomas struggled for a long time afterward until the Canada Southern and Great Western Railways established lines through the settlement. This resulted in a great surge of new business, employment and population. Both railway lines had to build high-level wooden trestles across Kettle Creek. The Canada Southern bridge was 1,300 feet long and 90 feet high. The Great Western bridge measured 900 feet in length and a height of 80 feet in the centre. Together they used almost a million board feet of timber.

One of the prominent citizens of St. Thomas in the early days was Edward Ermatinger of Swiss descent. Before he settled in St. Thomas in 1830, he had been a fur trader in the employ of the Hudson Bay Company. He turned to writing about the life of Colonel Talbot when he finally settled down and he later became a regular columnist for the Hamilton Spectator newspaper under the pseudonym of "A British Canadian". He died in 1876.

By the first half of the 20th century St. Thomas had numerous industries established here. The Ford Moter Company built an assembly plant just outside the city limits. Products from St. Thomas ranged from aircraft, automotive parts and machinery to nylons, woollens, shoes, plastics and metal signs.

St. Thomas is also the home of Alma College, a young ladies school, first established in 1881. The college was named by Sheriff Monroe of Elgin County after his wife and daughter, both of whom were called Alma.

The capital of Talbot's empire, St. Thomas today reflects a wealth of Victorian architecture, in particular, the city hall, the courthouse, Alma College and the old St. Thomas Church, vintage 1824. Just outside of the city, history buffs can view the Southwold Earthworks, a unique double-walled Neutral Indian fort. Only the earthwork remains, but the isolated position has a pronounced atmosphere.

Colonel Talbot may have taken a drink when the setting sun highlighted a small mark on the wall, but his vision for this city was clear-eyed and it shows today.

STONEY CREEK

The Gage homestead at Stoney Creek.

Women played an important role in Canadian history and some towns in Ontario can be thankful to a courageous woman for the actual origins of their settlement. Such is the case of Stoney Creek and its founding settler, Mary Gage.

Her story begins prior to the American revolution when she and her Welsh grandparents emigrated to America and settled on the bank of the Hudson River. Her husband was John Gage, an officer of an Irish Regiment stationed in the colony. John was killed in Wyoming and Mary was left to fend for herself and her son James, born in 1772, and her daughter Elizabeth, born in 1774. Discontent with war, she sought to live in peace. From Wyoming she set out on her long pilgrimage to the Niagara Peninsula. Accounts differ in regards to their style of transportation. Some say they travelled by canoe, other accounts say they came on horseback, but no matter how the journey was made, it was, nonetheless, remarkable for its courage and endurance.

In the Niagara Pennisula, Mary settled on land near a creek later named Stoney Creek, after the settlement by the same name. Mary's brother was the Deputy Land Surveyor, Augustus Jones. He had arrived here earlier and operated a farm at the south end of the beach. From 1787-1800, Jones surveyed many of the townships along Lake Ontario's northern shore, Dundas Street westward from York to London and Yonge Street northward from York to Lake Simcoe. He married the daughter of an Ojibway Chief and their son, the Reverend Peter Jones, became a famous Indian missionary who was perhaps better known as Sacred Feathers.

Mary, a young widow who had been left to her own resources, cleared her land, tilled the soil and cared for her children in a log cabin. The first log structure was replaced by a frame house which still stands today and is called The Battlefield House.

Mary's daughter Elizabeth was married in 1796 to Major Westbrook and they raised sixteen children. Mary's son James married Mary Davis that same year. James and his Loyalist wife from North Carolina lived with his mother in the Gage homestead.

James Gage prospered as a farmer and as a successful merchant. Southwest of the house he built a store and for many years this house and store were the only stopping places between Niagara and Ancaster.

In 1807, he made the first survey for a village on land he had purchased from Catharine Brant. This new village was first known as Wellington Square and later as Burlington.

James and Mary seldom closed their doors to strangers but on the night of June 5, 1813, the doors of the Gage house opened to the enemy. The War of 1812-14 had arrived at the settlement of Stoney Creek. An invading United States Army of about three thousand men occupied the house and camped in the vicinity. When seven hundred British regulars of the 8th and 49th regiments, under the command of Lieutenant-Colonel John Harvey, attacked the American force under cover of darkness, the women and children were locked in the cellar. James Gage was confined in a nearby hut and guarded by a sentry. In the confusion of the battle the sentry ran away and James escaped. He made for his house, to see to the safety of his family and as he crossed the field of fire several bullets pierced his hat. His loved ones were safe, and by sunrise the vanquished Americans had departed. Battlefield House was riddled with bullet holes.

Peter Jones or Sacred Feathers, as he was known among native people, had seen with his own eyes the carnage and destruction of war. He and his brother visited the battlefield the following day and described it as thick with dead men, horses, guns, swords, tents and baggage. He never forgot this scene. For the Mississaugas their hunting territory was devastated. The fairly isolated countryside that they trapped and hunted at leisure was invaded by over one thousand British soldiers, militiamen and Indian allies. In October of that year more than two thousand starving native refugees arrived in the Stoney Creek and Burlington area, looking for food. Their traditional way of life had come to an abrupt end as a direct result of the War of 1812.

It was not until 1913 that the Battle of Stoney Creek was commemorated by the unveiling of a monument in Battlefield Park. The unveiling was effected electronically, the impulse was triggered by a button located in London, England, and pushed on cue by Queen Mary of Britain.

Although the Gage family played a vital role in the development of the settlement of Stoney Creek, they were joined by other ambitious settlers. Jim Stoney, a trapper, and Edmund Stoney, an Anglican minister have been given credit for the name of the hamlet.

Stoney Creek grew slowly until 1840, when lake freight was first brought to the Stoney Creek docks. The village quickly became a major commercial centre for the region and a rival for Hamilton. Two large grain-storage warehouses were erected here to capture the grain market, although local businessmen eagerly anticipated the arrival of the railway. When the Great Western Railway did arrive in 1853, it ran instead to Hamilton and designated Stoney Creek only a station stop instead of a terminal. As a result of this decision, Hamilton gained the grain market and other industry as well, and Stoney Creek declined to become a quiet, rural centre.

In 1897, Stoney Creek became known as the birthplace of the Women's Institute. Erland Lee, one of the founders of the Farmer's Institute, his wife and Mrs. Adelaide Hoodless are credited with being the founders of this movement.

Stoney Creek was not officially an autonomous village until 1931. There was growth as a natural consequence of the commercial and industrial expansion of Hamilton. In time the boundaries between the two were indistinct and Stoney Creek became a residential area for Hamilton workers. In 1956, Stoney Creek achieved town status and elected William S. Milmine as its first mayor.

It is of interest to note that the city of Hamilton is flanked by Stoney Creek in the southeast and Dundas to the northwest and these communities were both settled by strong pioneering women – Mary Gage and Anne Morden, respectively.

TILLSONBURG

Iron ore deposits brought settlers to Tillsonburg. George Tillson from Enfield Massachusetts came to Upper Canada in 1822, and with three partners operated a pioneer foundry at Normandale in Norfolk County. In 1825, he sold his holdings and bought six hundred acres on Otter Creek with one of his former partners, Benjamin Van Norman, and together they built a dam, a sawmill and a new forge. Their forge melted and manufactured the bog iron ore deposits discovered in the area.

The settlement that grew up around this industry was called Dereham Forge and was later named Tillsonburg in honour of its original settler. Tillson set about surveying his land and erecting shanties to house the labourers working at the foundry. His partner, Van Norman, opened the first store in 1836 and organized the construction of a grist mill.

That same year, the settlers held a meeting and appointed George Tillson as commissioner of roads. He began immediately to improve the roads leading into Tillsonburg. He was the man who insisted on a one-hundred-foot-wide main street and to this day Tillsonburg has one of the widest main streets in Ontario.

E.D. Tillson, his sixth son, followed in his father's footsteps. In 1847, E.D. joined in partnership with Wright Barker and C. Codey and opened a sawmill. This business venture was the start of a milling complex that put Tillsonburg on the map. A 500-foot dam across Otter Creek, with several water races, provided sufficient power to operate the various industries in the area.

In 1865, Tillsonburg became a police village and it achieved town status in 1869.

By the 1890's E.D. Tillson owned many of the business interests in Tillsonburg. After his death in 1902, his empire quickly crumbled. His properties were sold and eventually his businesses were closed or destroyed by fire. The first library was housed in the old Mechanics Institute building in 1910 but the Carnegie Foundation supplied funds to allow construction of a real library in 1915.

Today Tillsonburg is situated in the heart of tobacco country. Like other small towns in Ontario, Tillsonburg owes a great deal to one or two enterprising pioneers who had a dream to build something that would continue after their demise. In this case it was a father and son whose dream happened to be a town and their dream is a reality – a town of 10,000 people.

TOBERMORY

One of Ontario's most unique historical and tourist attractions is situated under water. Fathom Five, Canada's only underwater park is located at Tobermory. This park offers beginner and advanced scuba divers sea caves and nineteen shipwrecks to see and explore. Fathom Five is a unique park developed to introduce the visitor to the educational values and recreational opportunities of an aquatic environment.

The forty-five square mile park extends from the land base of the Niagara Escarpment to the Cape Hurd Islands. During the 1850's, the waters around the pennisula became an important trade and transportation route. This increase in shipping led to the establishment of major navigational aids such as Cove Island Lighthouse in 1855. Big Tub Lighthouse in 1885 and Flowerpot Island Lighthouse in 1897. Even with these additional aids many of the vessels rounding the tip of the pennisula went to the bottom during a gale or ran aground on an island during a thick fog. Although nineteen shipwrecks exist in the park, further documentation indicates that several other shipwrecks exist in the area, but have not been found.

These shipwrecks represent a good cross-section of sail and steam vessels dating from the mid-19th century. The schooner Philo Scoville, built in Cleveland, Ohio, in 1863, went down during a storm in October of 1899 off Russel Island. Today pieces of the wreck rest in twenty-five feet to ninety-five feet of water. The bow portion can be found at the deeper depths and the anchors are located about one hundred feet east of the main wreckage. This site is recommended to persons with advanced levels of diving experience.

An excellent site for snorkelers and novice divers is the wreck of John Walters. This schooner, built in 1852, at Kingston, was wrecked about the same time as the Philo Scoville and sits in fifteen feet of water.

For the photographer and botanist a multitude of wild flowers can be found throughout the land base, including several varieties of orchids and ferns. Anyone interested in geology would be interested to examine the flowerpot formations that have been created by the intense water activity at the base of resistant strata within the cliff of Flowerpot Island.

Boat tours offer a delightful view of shipwrecks from the safety of a glass bottomed boat. Several local captains operate a fleet for charter and sightseeing cruises of the park.

The village of Tobermory, named by the Scottish fishermen from the Isle of Mull, was first settled in 1871 by Captain John Charles Earl. Like a fishing village of the east coast, the village offers a quaint atmosphere of hospitality that is definitely Canadian.

A thirty-minute walking tour of Tobermory is a must. Many of the original homesteads still dot the shore of one of Georgian Bay's finest natural harbours. According to tradition a permanent commercial fishery was formed at Tobermory in 1884. An old boiler house once stood on the west side of the harbour where the new crib dock now stands. It was later used an an ice-house and net shed. From the early to the mid-1900's tons of marketable lake trout were drawn from the waters surrounding Tobermory. Many a resident of the village depended on fishing for a livelihood.

Tobermory also serves as the launching spot for thousands of hikers bent on travelling the Bruce Trail, the northern section of which is considered to include the most spectacular scenery of the entire trail.

The two harbours of Tobermory, known as Big Tub and Little Tub, serve as marine centres for the northern part of the Peninsula. From Big Tub, Tobermory to South Bay Mouth, Manitoulin Island, passengers and vehicles are transported twice a day from May to October. This provides a scenic opportunity to travel across Georgian Bay instead of around it and renders Tobermory a watery doorway to the north.

WALKERTON

Four native boys having a puff of tobacco.

Late one afternoon in the spring of 1849, as the sun was setting in the west, Thomas Adair stood looking out over the most beautiful landscape he had ever beheld. From the vision it inspired, a tiny settlement began to grow by the waters edge; in this place that the Indians called Hahskosesing, meaning "a little marsh", Walkerton began to emerge.

The following year, William Jasper and Edward Boulton followed Adair's footsteps and erected the first house east of the river. The site of this log shanty stood at the intersection of Bay and Mary Streets and Durham Road.

In 1850, Joseph Walker arrived and constructed a dam across the Saugeen and then erected mills to cut lumber and grind flour for the scattered settlers. Realizing the potential for a town to grow here, he had the adjacent farm lots surveyed into a town plot. Walker's log home not only served to shelter his family, but to house visitors to the new community. His house stood at what is now the intersection of Durham and Mill Streets.

Two years later, a post office was opened in John Sheenan's store, a post office labelled Brant, after the township. In 1857, the post office name was changed to Walkerton in honour of the founder of the settlement.

Joseph Walker was a man of vision who worked for nine years to have Walkerton selected as a county town. In 1865, his ambition was realized, Walkerton was selected and the county buildings were erected. At the time, Walkerton did not have a large enough population to claim incorporation as a village. However, because the community was selected as the county town, a special Act of Parliament was passed on February 15, 1871, to enable Walkerton to assume the dignity of a town without ever having been a village municipality.

The man, called Old Joe (Walker) by many, was from the County of Tyrone, Ireland and emigrated to Cookstown as a young boy. When he entered the County of Bruce he was forty-nine.

The founder of Walkerton was rather careless in business and as a result most of his assets were lost by 1870. Undaunted, he gathered everything together and left to make a fresh start on Manitoulin Island. Once there, he purchased a mill privilege and erected a grist mill at the Sheguindah village. He died at age seventy-two in the year 1873.

For a number of years, the only manufacturing industries that existed in the town were sawmills and grist mills. In 1864, James Blair opened a foundry and machine shop where the present town hall stands. The plant ran successfully for several years until it fell prey to fire in May of 1877. A woollen mill and a felt-boot factory existed for a period of time and then disappeared.

Walkerton, like many other Ontario towns, fell victim to fire. On May 28, 1877, early in the afternoon a fire began in a stable situated behind the site of the present post office. Due to a high wind, the fire swept over a large part of the business section of town. The losses were heavy, forty-two buildings were destroyed. People worked frantically to rebuild their town. The new buildings appeared finer and had more architectural character than those they were replacing.

For a town once viewed as a northern settlement, Walkerton's isolation was short-lived. In 1868, the wires of the Montreal Telegraph Company reached town. Sixteen years later, the Bell Telephone Company arrived. That same year, 1884, as residents chatted to distant relations, Arc Electric lamps were installed in the streets, churches and shops of Walkerton.

Fortunately, Walkerton still maintains a number of handsome period buildings. Two that were erected by the municipality include the town hall built in 1897 and a fine building used as the post office, customs and inland revenue offices in 1890.

The streets are still adorned with shade trees, thanks to a town council who, on June 18, 1877, passed a bylaw offering to pay twenty-five cents, on certain conditions, for each tree planted along the streets of the town. Sidewalks in the early days consisted of plank platforms placed in front of each shop. These wooden sidewalks on the various streets extended several miles. In 1891, the first granolithic walk was installed by the post office. By 1905, more than five miles of sidewalk had been put down across town.

The oldest athletic sport in Walkerton is curling. First started in February 1870, the curling club soon became quite prominent in the district. Prior to this the curlers played on the ice covering the mill-pond. The curling stones were blocks of wood, turned, when possible, from a large knot. To these were attached iron handles made by the local smith. The curling stones, quite clumsy to carry, were left on the ice after the close of each game. This practice was done once too often. One winter day a thaw came, and ice and curling stones together went over the dam and disappeared down the river. The curlers soon changed locations to the old drill shed.

Since 1900, a number of industries have disappeared. Among these are the Rattan Factory where baby buggies, chairs and tables were made. A binder twine factory, three brickyards, three tanneries, two flour and grist mills, five tailor shops, two dressmaking shops, three jewellery shops, and four blacksmith shops have all closed their doors. The industries that have arrived to replace them include Bogdon and Gross Furniture, Canada Packers Limited, Canada Spool and Bobbin, and Union Carbide.

The Bruce Nuclear Power Station on Lake Huron to the west has attracted newcomers for whom it is no problem to commute a short distance to work when the traffic is minimal. This has given support to small businesses and development in the downtown sector as well as provided a cultural influence from city- oriented residents.

WALLACEBURG

Sales and Feed barn in Wallaceburg, c. 1900.

Wallaceburg was once called "The Forks" for its location at the junction of the north and east branches of the Sydenham River. Most inhabitants of The Forks had come from the nearby Baldoon settlement of Lord Selkirk. They were forced to abandon Baldoon after frequent flooding of their low-lying lands. Numerous accounts of malaria and the theft of livestock by American militia invaders in the War of 1812, forced many to move. Another reason seldom mentioned but occasionally told as a hearth-side story on long winter nights, was the story of the Baldoon Mysteries.

It was the summer of 1829 when John McDonald married. He and his wife built a lovely frame house in the settlement of Baldoon, near Wallaceburg. John's house was coveted by a family known as the People of the Long Low House. They approached him with offers to purchase. He refused and to this owed all the miseries he came to endure.

It all began the day the men went off to their farm duties and the women gathered in the pole barn for their afternoon work. As the girls sat chatting they were startled by the sudden displacement of and fall of a roof pole. Suddenly another crashed to the floor. When a third pole came thundering down, the ladies fled for the house. Once inside they were startled again when a shower of bullets came threw the window.

For three successive years this afflicted family were to be the victims of many such manifestations. The placement of some strong inch boards over the windows did not stop the bullets from passing through. In time, little balls of fire began to float in the air and settle in various parts of the house. Then, one day fire razed the McDonald home to the ground. John and his family moved to his father's house, but soon the hauntings resumed. John was desperate. He went to visit a girl who had second sight. She told him it was all due to the people of The Long Low House, to return home and find a black goose and shoot it. She continued to say that the destroyer of your peace takes the shape of that bird. If you wound it, your enemy, too, will be wounded.

McDonald eventually found the black goose down by the river and shot it. The bullet struck the bird and broke its wing. John turned his footsteps towards The Long Low House. One anxious look revealed all. There sat the old woman of the house with a broken arm, uttering curses. For John McDonald and his family, no spiritual manifestations were heard of again.

James Johnson was the first pioneer who 'squatted' at the present site of Wallaceburg in 1809. He built a trading post at what became known as Johnson's Point.

The McDougall family are considered to be the founders of Wallaceburg. A survey done in 1821 shows that Laughlin McDougall settled east of the junction of the Sydenham River and Bear Creek. There he erected a log tavern and trading post. Eventually McDougall constructed a large frame building and made schooners.

Hugh McCallum arrived sometime near 1832 and in 1836 surveyed the land south of the Forks. McCallum was the one who gave the settlement the name of Wallaceburg, after the Scottish hero, Sir William Wallace.

Wallaceburg's growth was spurred on by the lumber business, and the navigable rivers of the area. By 1846, the settlement became a port of entry with Colonel John Bell as customs agent. The banks of the river were lined with docking facilities and storehouses. A substantial ship-building industry was operating by the late eighteen hundreds, dominated by one of Wallaceburg's leading citizens, Captain James W. Steinhoff.

In 1873, Wallaceburg became a village and by 1896, was incorporated as a town. Local agriculture was given a boost when a large sugar refinery opened in Wallaceburg in 1900 and industry was encouraged when William Taylor proposed a glass manufacturing plant. The venture was a success because of the promotional support it received and the convenience of deep-water navigation for transportation. A variety of other industries responded to this successful development. The major attraction was the excellent shipping facilites, both by rail and by water and eventually the industries included a brass plant, an iron foundry, a furniture factory, a creamery and a pressure-cooker manufacturer.

The town remains an industrial and agricultural centre for the area. Local features include parks, a glass factory outlet and a public docking facility for 200 boats on the Sydenham River. Like many Ontario communities, Wallaceburg had some noteworthy citizens within its population. One such resident was James R. Lee, the inventor of the Lee rifle, and forerunner of the Lee-Enfield; another was Jeanne (Ruby) Gordon, a celebrated opera singer in her time. Oh, and, of course, one was a black goose!

WASAGA BEACH

As Schooner Town and as a naval establishment on Lake Huron from 1812-1815, Wasaga Beach played an important role in the War of 1812.

It was here that the schooner, Nancy, built in 1789, was pressured into military service during the war. She was used to carry supplies north to Fort Michilimackinac and on one of these trips the Nancy was pursued two miles up the Nottawasaga River by three American vessels. Lieutenant Worsley, who was in command, refused to admit defeat although the odds were overwhelmingly against him. The Nancy had only three guns and a crew of twenty- three compared to the twenty-four guns and five hundred crewmen on the American vessels. Despite the odds, Worsley turned to fight the enemy who quickly sank the Nancy, but not before the Lieutenant and his crew succeeded in departing the ship and in securing their supplies in the bush. Shortly thereafter reinforcements arrived from St. Joseph's and Worsley struck out against the enemy once more. This time he seized two of the American schooners.

Reid and Ayling's "Trail of the Caribou", 1934.

An accumulation of silt over the years has covered the sunken hull of the Nancy and in time has created an island by the same name. This island today supports a museum commemorating those early days, a lighthouse and a theatre.

At the entrance to Nancy Island there is an historic plaque dedicated to the first manned flight from the mainland of Canada to England. It was from Wasaga Beach, on the morning of the 8th of August, 1934, that James R. Ayling and Leonard G. Reid took off in their plane, "The Trail of the Caribou", bound for Baghdad. Adverse weather conditions and a shortage of fuel forced them to land at Heston Airfield in London, England on the afternoon of the 9th of August; they flew 3,700 miles in thirty hours and fifty-five minutes.

Wasaga Beach sports a magnificent strip of fine, sandy beach curving in a seven-mile-long cresent around the southeastern corner of Nottawasaga Bay, and extends inland along the Nottawasaga River. In the background, Blue Mountain towers a thousand feet above the water.

Before the turn of the century, nearby residents frequented Wasaga Beach by horse and buggy to picnic and to swim. By 1925 there were hundreds of cottages on the beach, 3,000 to 4,000 cars, and 15,000 people on any given sunny, summer Sunday. Two years later those figures, on a holiday weekend, increased to the 40,000 mark.

While other beach invasions took place during World War Two, so did the invasion of Wasaga Beach. Canada's large military base, Camp Borden, located not far from Wasaga, drew soldiers to Wasaga Beach and to its dance halls, to its honky-tonks and to tourist cabins for weekend recreation. Crowds were often estimated as high as 100,000 on a weekend during the war, and were even larger after the declaration of peace.

Weekend traffic continued to increase into the 1950's. More and more hotels opened up in Simcoe County, particularly around centres like Wasaga Beach. The demand for cottages increased and real estate developers bought up miles of lake-front property and divided it into small lots. The endless stretches of over-crowded shoreline began to resemble suburban streets.

Post-war prosperity saw improved highways in Simcoe County and faster cars on the road. Residents of Toronto and other metropolitan centres began to feel the need to get out into the country. The increased affluence and shorter work-weeks gave way to more leisure and the indulgence of country retreats.

Today Wasaga Beach might be called a "strip". There are several miles of inumerable, garishly decorated emporiums, bowling alleys, tourist

The Capstan Inn at Wasaga Beach, c. 1939.

cabins, motels, taverns, amusement arcades, miniature golf courses and dozens of restaurants. Some say it is Coney Island, Atlantic City and Toronto's old Sunnyside all rolled into one.

In 1959, following representations to the provincial government by the village of Wasaga Beach, an area was designated for a provincial park, which grew to a size of over 3,000 acres by the 1970's. The Ontario Lands and Forests, in 1962, limited access to the park and beach area to four controlled entrances. Wasaga Beach still works to maintain a balance in what the environment can handle in terms of people. There are no schooners to contend with but there still is the military and an ever-increasing number of tourists.

WATERLOO

The township of Waterloo was at one time one of the largest townships in southwestern Ontario. It was named in 1817 in commemoration of the victory of the British over Napolean at Waterloo. Joseph Brant, acting for the Six Nations Indians, sold 94,012 acres to Richard Beasley, James Wilson and Jean Baptiste Rosseaux in 1798.

In 1800, Beasley began to sell his land to immigrants of German decent from Pennsylvania. A handful of fur trappers lived along the Grand River in temporary homes that had been left by the first settlers. By 1802 new Mennonite settlers discovered that the deeds to their land were worthless. Beasley had not been the sole owner of the land. James Wilson and Jean Rosseaux also held title to the land that was already heavily mortgaged.

In 1804, Joseph Bricker and Joseph Sherk left for Pennsylvania to persuade friends and relatives to buy land in Waterloo for $20,000. Thanks to John Eby, a joint-stock company known as the German Company was formed with Bricker as appointed agent and Daniel Erb as his assistant.

The men did raise the money and returned by wagon with the cash wrapped in bags. (The same wagon can be seen today in the Waterloo County Museum.) In the meantime, Beasley had raised the purchase

Horse and buggy travelling down the road in Waterloo.

price to $40,000. Fortunately, a new wave of immigration from Pennsylvania to Waterloo insured the completion of the land deal.

Augustus Jones surveyed the township in 1806. New lots of land were laid out in an irregular manner to prevent interference with the property rights of established settlers. The old pioneer trails were kept and are visible today in the meandering streets of present-day Waterloo.

The first man to settle on this site was Abraham Erb in 1806. Erb had purchased his property from the German Company. First he built a sawmill and then in 1816 a grist mill. This was a relief to settlers in the area who had been travelling to Dundas for their flour. Although Erb provided accommodations for travellers in the basement of his mill, he refused to sell any of his land for lots to provide growth for a settlement.

Jacob C. Snider did buy the grist mill and the sawmill along with 240 acres of the Erb land in 1829. Improvements by Snider, such as a steam power plant and distillery, encouraged more people to settle in the area. His son, Elias, sold the property in 1854 to Isaac Weber and John Hoffman who opened the land up for settlement.

A community grew up around the mills. In 1831, a post office opened and between 1835 and 1855, a large number of immigrants arrived. The Kuntz family settled here in 1844 and established a brewery that was a forerunner of Carling's Brewery.

By 1851, the population of Waterloo exceeded 250. Over the next few years, stagecoach lines made transportation easier and brought more settlers to the area. The population of Waterloo reached 1,400 by 1855. The community now had two sawmills, a flour mill, a foundry, a cabinet factory, a small weaving mill, a potter's shop, a distillery, a brewery, a harness shop, and a tree and garden nursery. Two years later Waterloo incorporated as a village.

A new type of industry began in Waterloo in the 1860's – the insurance business. The Waterloo Mutual Fire Insurance Company was founded in 1863 by Cyrus M. Taylor. By the late nineteenth century, the company had agencies throughout the province. Cyrus Taylor also established the Ontario Mutual Life Assurance Company, which would later become Mutual Life of Canada. After the growth of a number of insurance companies Waterloo became known as "the Hartford of Canada."

Joseph E. Seagram purchased a partnership in a local distillery in 1870, and eventually took over the entire operation. This was the beginning of Seagram Distilleries. The Seagram family later contributed substantially to the development of Waterloo – they sponsored a band, donated land to see the erection of a hospital and provided employment for many townspeople. It was a horse from the Seagram stables that won the Queen's Plate in 1891, and then went on to win championships eight times in a row.

With a population close to 2,000, in 1876, Waterloo was incorporated as a town. A new town council was formed and quickly set about promoting the building of railways. By 1877, an agreement had been reached with the Grand Trunk Railway to bring a line to Waterloo. The town continued to operate as the terminus of the railway until 1889 when it was extended to Elmira. The Canadian Pacific also provided a line to Waterloo and a street railway became a reality in 1890 that linked Waterloo and Berlin (Kitchener).

The town's population reached 4,000 by 1906. Industries included the Waterloo Manufacturing Comapny, a world leader in the manufacture of threshing machinery. There was the J.B. Snider Company that manufactured office, school and church furniture. The Union Mills shipped flour all over Canada and to Britain. Bechtels' brickmaking establishment quickly rose to become Canada's leading brickmaker and refiners in the area of brickmaking machinery.

The Inn along the side of the road.

In 1911 the Evangelical Lutheran Seminary was opened in Waterloo. In 1924 it became the Waterloo College, a liberal arts college affiliated with the University of Western Ontario. In 1959 it was renamed Waterloo Lutheran University and in the 1970's the name was changed to Wilfrid Laurier University. The University is the largest engineering school with co-operative industrial work-study programs in Canada.

The establishment of new industries was encouraged in 1910 when Waterloo became one of the first municipalities in the province to receive power from Niagara. Waterloo continued to grow and was incorporated as a city in 1948. Today Kitchener and Waterloo connect so closely that people often refer to them as the "Twin Cities".

For years Waterloo has been known for its musical traditions. The first Saengerfest in Canada, a major choir and band festival was held in 1874. The event became so popular that a special arena was constructed in Berlin (Kitchener) for the annual event. A Waterloo Musical Society was formed in 1882 and their band, led by Noah Zellar, caused such a stir that Joseph Seagram was inspired to donate a band shell in the town square for concerts. In 1932, the Waterloo Band Festival was started.

In 1969 Waterloo and Kitchener held Oktoberfest celebrations during mid-October. The event was so popular that the Twin Cities made it an annual event. The festival has now become the largest one of its kind in North America, attracting more than 350,000 people annually. There are over thirty festival halls and tents with beer, sausage, sauerkraut, and oompah music in the best Bavarian tradition.

Another great attraction to visit in Waterloo is the Seagram Museum. The museum captures the history and technology of the wine and spirits industry with artifacts from around the world. It is housed in the original Seagram distillery barrel warehouse.

Joseph Brant and the early settlers felt this area had much to offer and so it does.

✿

WELLAND

The completion of the first Welland Canal in 1829 marked the beginnings of new settlement along its course. The city of Welland owes its very existence to this canal.

The story of Welland begins with the construction of a wooden feeder canal. It supplied water from the Grand River, twenty miles to the southwest, across the Chippawa Creek by means of a huge wooden aqueduct to supply the canal. A settlement grew up here around this structure, and was first known as the hamlet of Aqueduct. Businesses and individuals were drawn here because the canal by-passed their original places of residence.

In 1842, Aqueduct was renamed Merrittsville in honour of William Hamilton Merritt, the financial agent for and promoter of The Welland Canal Company. Many of the people who settled in Merrittsville were the labourers who worked on the canal. A large number of these men were Irish immigrants and escaped slaves from the United States. That same year, the Welland Canal Company decided to replace the entire wooden canal with one of stone.

Labourers of the Welland Canal worked from sun-up to sun-down. A typical morning scene would begin at camp – a bell would ring and one thousand workers would rise up and head out to work with a hundred teams of horses and oxen. Progress was slow with delays caused by fire, poor drinking water, fights among the men and labour strikes for higher

The Welland Canal.

wages. Threat of death was always present as disease and over-exertion claimed many lives. This massive engineering feat, that demanded so much human strength and horsepower, was first completed in 1850. By then the permanent population of Merrittsville was one hundred and fifty. Industries in the settlement included two sawmills, two grist mills and a cloth factory.

In 1858, Merrittsville was incorporated as a village and the name was changed to that of the river. The Welland River had been named by Governor Simcoe after the Welland River in Lincolnshire, England.

Welland's early economy was based largely on the existence of the canal. Horses were in great demand for towing vessels along the canal, and so stables were quite the lucrative enterprise. Much of the timber used on various stages of the canal was cut locally and floated down the canal to be milled. The shipbuilding industry flourished during this period because of the demand created by the new waterway. Welland was selected in 1855 as the judicial seat of Welland County. The following year a massive stone county court house, designed in the Renaissance style by noted Toronto architect, Kivas Tully, was constructed at a cost of more than $100,000.

Immigrant workers enjoying a day in town.

In 1878, Welland was incorporated as a town. A swing bridge across the canal linked the town, which was situated on both sides of the waterway. The third Welland Canal was opened in 1887. The channel of the second canal had been widened by then, the route of the first canal had been filled in and a stone adqueduct had been constructed to the west of the first one. One year later, much to the relief of the townspeople, the installation of a waterworks was underway. Prior to this, residents had to drink unfiltered water from the canal, which often contained mud and minute aquatic creatures.

In 1913, the construction of a fourth Welland commenced, but was interrupted by World War One. Work resumed shortly after the war and was completed in 1932. The new canal was capable of handling vessels up to 730 feet long and with cargo loads that weighed 28,000 tons. The canal consisted of eight locks and measured a depth of twenty-seven feet. The earlier canals had been a system of aqueducts which were then eliminated. Welland's main street crossed the canal by a single lift-bridge. It is interesting to note that every time the canal was reconstructed the layout of the town was altered.

During the summer of 1913, fire gutted the upper part of the Welland County Building. The following year the building was reopened after extensive restoration. It was during this period of time that heavy industry began to locate at Welland. The pace of industrialization increased following both wars and among the companies that established here were the Welland Iron and Brass Company, Canadian Mead-Morrison Company, Welland Electric Steel Foundry, Dominion Yarns, Atlas Steels, Stokes Rubber Company, and Commonwealth Electric. By the end of World War Two the population of Welland had reached 16,000, but annexation of township property in 1961 and again in 1970 pushed the population to 45,505.

Welland lies in the heart of a prosperous agriculture region. It has excellent transportation facilities and a convenient power supply from Niagara Falls. These factors have helped to sustain it as a manufacturing centre that continues to make steel products, textiles, fertilizer and processed agricultural products.

Today the city of Welland is not only known for shipping and its steel industry, but for roses. For many, Welland is called the Rose City. Each year in June, the Welland Rose Festival, a two-week event, focuses on the roses grown in the area. Roses are judged and graded. Parades, boat races and a coronation ball are just a few of the other festivities planned each year.

Welland had the key to the development of the shipping industry from Lake Ontario to Lake Erie. What more appropriate place to hold such a key than a city full of locks?

The Welland County Courthouse.

WIARTON

A Native village near Wiarton, c. 1870.

The unique setting and beauty of Wiarton places it first among the other towns of the County of Bruce. None other can compare with its picturesque quality and the haunting accounts of early shipping days on Georgian Bay. The view from the hill at the south of Wiarton charms every visitor as they approach the town; it extends for miles down Colpoy's Bay with White Cloud and Hay Islands in the distance; bold limestone cliffs just out and extend as far as the eye can see along the west shore.

Unlike most localities in the County of Bruce, Wiarton has its very own Indian legend entitled "The Spirit Rock." Situated between Wiarton and Whicher's Point, The Spirit Rock can be seen quite distinctly from the bay. As the legend goes the daughter of a chief of one of the tribes whose hunting ground was in the immediate vicinity of Colpoy's Bay, was carried off by an Eastern tribe. They bore her miles away and condemned her to a life of drudgery because she was the daughter of a hated foe. The Eastern Chieftain passed one day while she was singing a sad, plaintive song. The song and the youth and beauty of the maiden awakened feelings of admiration and love in this chieftain's breast. He released her from her bondage, and with simple rites the chief and maiden were wed. The warriors of the tribe were angered at this union and plotted to destroy it. So effective were they that dire disaster met the bride and her consort. Her warrior chief was stricken from her side, but she escaped and wandered back to her own tribe, arriving weary and footsore only to be refused admittance into the band. By becoming the willing bride of their deadly foe, she had brought dishonour upon herself. A poem best describes the rest of the story.

> For hours he stood upon that rocky height
> Till night's dark curtain had shut out the light,
> Then, with a cry like a lost soul in woe,
> She sprang to her death and her grave below,
> While moaning winds murmured a funeral strain,
> And sighing waves echoed a sad refrain.

On the face of the cliff, standing out in bold relief, the crevices and stains depict a woman's face above a pine tree.

Oxenden seems to have been the first place on the bay to be settled. Soon another group of settlers took up land at Colpoy's Bay. Wiarton town lots were not offered for sale until 1868. And when they were the original cost of these lots was $6.00, subsequently raised to $10.00, and then to $40.00.

James Lennox was the first pioneer to arive and build a log shanty on November 16, 1866, at what is now Wiarton. The absence of a wharf or facilities for shipping resulted in the nucleus of the town being founded on top of the hill. The business centre of the community was situated at the corner where Gould Street is crossed by Division Street.

In 1868, B.B. Miller, born in Kircudbrightshire, Scotland, settled here, built a hotel and opened a post office. In the same year the Indian Department offered a $300 grant to the settlement to build a wharf. Once the wharf was operative, a steamer from Collingwood named the Hero called once or twice a week. Service improved by 1869 when the steamer Champion made daily trips to Owen sound and provided a regular link for Wiarton with the outside world. Wiarton quickly became the sole market town for a substantial stretch of the county.

Wiarton was incorporated as a village on March 5, 1880 with a population of 752 settlers. After the wharves were constructed and mills erected below the hill, the places of business moved to Berford Street and by 1889, Gould Street became largely residential.

Colpoy's Bay has had its share of marine disasters. The best remembered and talked about is that of the loss of the Jane Miller, which occurred November 25, 1881. The Jane Miller, built in 1879, was a Wiarton boat owned by Captain Andrew Port.

The story begins when she departed Owen Sound under threatening skies. Sailing east, she stopped at Meaford to take on additional freight and passengers and cleared for the Bruce Peninsula. On board was Captain Port, mate Richard Port, purser Fred Port, engineer S. Christison, wheelsman Alexander Scales, and four deck hands. Nearly thirty passengers, including one Captain Malcolm McLeod of Goderich and a group of workmen bound for Watt's Mill at Lions Head and McLander's lumber shanty at Tobermory, waited anxiously to arrive safely at Wiarton.

The Jane Miller ploughed through heavy seas and arrived around 8:30 in the evening at Big Bay to wood up. It was at this time that Captain Port was overheard to say how severely his vessel was rolling and that she was shipping considerable water. The wood supply at Big Bay was insufficient so the Captain ordered the wheelsman to steer the boat towards Spencer's Dock, another fueling point on the east shore of Colpoy's Bay less than eight miles from Wiarton. The eastern passage into Colpoy's Bay lies through a mile-wide strait between White Cloud Island and Cameron Point. At the latter place Roderick Cameron and his wife stood on the shore in expectation of seeing the steamer Wiarton Belle which was to bring their son from Owen Sound to Wiarton. Instead, at 9 p.m., with a southwest gale blowing, they spotted the Jane Miller, her light glowing through the swirling snow as she entered the jaws of the storm. They watched as the vessel struggled nearing Spencer's Dock, just two miles distance. As the Jane Miller made her final approach, her lights suddenly went out, and she was never seen again. Several days later some wreckage of the ship washed ashore at Hay Island, north of White Cloud, but no survivors were ever found.

On January 1, 1894, the residents of Wiarton were numerous enough to take unto themselves the privileges and honours of a town. It is interesting to note that the gentlemen who surveyed the town plot of Wiarton named many of the streets after themselves and their wives. The community received its name from the birthplace of Sir Edmund Walker Head, Governor-General at the time of its survey, who was born at Wiarton Place near Maidstone, Kent, England.

Among the principal industries in operation around the turn of the century were furniture factories, a large fish packing plant and a beet sugar manufacturing plant. The beet sugar plant ran into financial

Barn raising at Wiarton c. 1900.

difficulties after only three seasons. The Table Factory burned down in 1916 and just a few years later a similar fate struck The Chair Factory.

There are no longer any great quantities of timber or fish shipped out of Wiarton by train. Passenger service came to an end on the railway in 1959, and the railway station closed completely in 1968. The lumber industry disappeared when forests diminished from fires and over-zealous harvests and when competition became more fierce.

In 1934, The Wiarton Board of Trade saw the potential for tourist development. A Survey made at that time indicated that there were 750 cottages in the area, but by 1968 the number had increased to upwards of 5,000. Extensive advertising with brochures depicting golf courses, tennis courts,a dance hall, boat races and sport fishing gave Wiarton the push it needed to become a flourishing tourist attraction.

WINDSOR

An abandoned log cabin at Windsor.

The city of Windsor is located on the south bank of the Detroit River opposite the American city of Detroit. It grew on the site of the oldest permanent settlement in Upper Canada. Missionaries first arrived here in 1640. A fur trading post, operating during French rule, stood on the east side of the Detroit River. A fortified post called Fort Pontchartrain welcomed French settlers here in 1734. Some twenty years later at the time of the British Conquest, several hundred settlers were scattered along the river. When the British surrendered Detroit to the Americans in 1794, they withdrew from the garrison and were followed by several Americans to the Canadian side to establish the settlement of Sandwich.

This new community supplanted Detroit as the capital of the Western District. The British even moved an abandoned Blockhouse to the vicinity of present-day Brock and Sandwich Streets to serve as a court-house and gaol. Unfortunately, it was gutted by fire in 1799 and replaced by another structure which was destroyed by the Americans during the War of 1812. A third courthouse on the same site remained until 1855, when The Essex County Courthouse was built, and remained operational until the 1960's.

A townsite was laid out at a ferry crossing, opposite the foot of Woodward Avenue. In 1835, the public gathered at Hutton's Tavern to choose a name for the new site. James Dougall suggested the name Windsor, after the Town of Windsor, England. It was agreed and to commemorate this historic event the owner of the tavern also renamed his establishment. It became "Windsor Castle".

Many of the early French families carried names like Baby, Dumouchelle, Goyeau, Jannesse, Langlois, and Meloch. The first brick home was built on the Baby farm. It was still standing during the War of 1812 and it played a significant part. General Hull made this house his headquarters during his invasion of Canada in 1812. In 1813, the house served as headquarters for General Harrison while he pursued General Proctor.

Windsor in the early days was always a source of dissent among the French, British and Americans. They all had interests in Windsor due to its crucial position on the Detroit River. Windsor even played a vital role in the Rebellion of Upper Canada. In the early morning of December 4, 1838, a force of 140 American and Canadian supporters of the Mackenzie Rebellion crossed the river from Detroit and took possession of Windsor. They were soon routed by militiamen under the command of Colonel John Prince. During the Colonel's attack, a number of the invaders were captured. Orders went out to execute four traitors and a violent stir of controversy began on both sides of the border. Six more prisoners were tried at London and sentenced to death. Some of the remaining captives were transported to a penal colony in Tasmania, and others were deported to the United States.

Up to the time of 1854, Windsor had not shown a great deal of promise for growth and development. However, that all changed when the community was selected to be the western terminus of the railway. A steam passenger ferry operating from Windsor to Detroit was responsible for this decision. This allowed for a connection with the Michigan Central Railway on the American side. A paddlewheeler named Union was later put in service and it transported a trainload of passengers on a single trip. Subsequently, a car ferry with two tracks was used to transport an entire train across water. In 1870, the Great Western and the Michigan Central Railway obtained power to build a railway tunnel under the Detroit River.

In 1858, Windsor became a town. By 1881, the population had

reached 7,000. Seven churches served the spiritual needs of the community. St. Alphonsus Roman Catholic Church was the largest and most expensive. St. Mary's Academy for young ladies had an enrollment of three hundred pupils in Windsor and Sandwich. The University of Windsor originates from the Roman Catholic Assumption College founded in 1857.

In March of 1855 a Detroit businessman, by the name of Hiram Walker, closed the door to his distillery at 35 Atwater Street, walked down to the river and gazed across at Windsor. A month earlier the Michigan Legislature had passed the Maine Law, which outlawed all liquor traffic. This was the temperance movement. Hiram Walker needed to relocate and Canada was the place.

He arrived in Windsor and purchased a large acreage east of the village of Windsor. In 1858, he built a distillery and called it the Windsor Distillery and Flouring Mill (later to become Hiram Walker and Sons Ltd). Soon industries began to locate around the Walker distillery. This area was beginning to be known as Walkerville. By 1869 it was official, Ottawa declared Walkerville to be a post-office village on its own.

By 1892, Windsor officially became a city. It was only in 1935 that the amalgamation of East Windsor, Walkerville, Windsor and Sandwich formed the greater City of Windsor.

During the 1920's Windsor followed the lead of Detroit and established a large automobile manufacturing centre. The proximity of Windsor to Detroit plants assisted greatly in the development of the industry. The completion of the Windsor- Detroit Tunnel, a vehicular tunnel leading into the heart of downtown Windsor on November 30, 1930, assisted in the growth of the automobile industry. Nearly a mile in length, the maximum depth of the roadway beneath the river surface is seventy-five feet.

A year before the completion of the underwater tunnel, the Ambassador Bridge was officially opened. It is the longest international suspension bridge in the world, stretching one and three quarter miles in length.

A very special historical event occurred in Windsor during the winter of 1937-38. Wa-Sha-Quon-Asin, (He-Who-Flies-By-night) Grey Owl, appeared at the King Edward Public School. One of Canada's greatest conservationists, Grey Owl spoke to the pupils seated on the floor of the kindergarden-auditorium. He pleaded for a way of life which was being eliminated by the callous progress of the white man. He began with these words, "I come to tell you that the animals of the forest are your friends".

Militia unit, c. 1866.

He had an incredible appeal for children, reaching them as no other teacher had before. Later he met with principals of the schools in the area at the Norton Palmer Hotel before he continued on with his crusade throughout Canada. He subsequently returned to his rustic cabin in the Prince Albert National Park, where he passed over exhausted, on April 13, 1938, five months before his fiftieth birthday.

During the depression of the 1930's a mass exodus from Windsor left twelve per-cent of the housing vacant. With the onset of the war, workers returned once again and there was then a housing shortage. Automobile plants were converted to manufacture war machinery. Farmers adjacent to the city increased production and canning industries added to the growing number of enterprises.

By 1950, manufacturing plants dominated the economy of Windsor. Foremost in this once again, was the automobile industry. A hydro-electric generating station was built in 1952- 54. Post-war years brought an influx of various ethnic groups, including Germans, Italians, Poles, Ukrainians, Czechs and Hungarians.

Several major railways and highways converge at Windsor and trade with the United States and domestic markets has a major effect on economy. Windsor's harbour facilities serve commercial fishing and handle imports of coal and freight. A position on the international border and on the Great Lakes affords a direct route to the Atlantic seaboard. Many manufacturers saw the potential of this and, as a result, Windsor is one of the great industrial cities of Canada.

Today, the visitor to Windsor has the opportunity to view several historic and cultural sites. The Art Gallery of Windsor, situated in a former brewers' warehouse, is worth a stop. The Hiram Walker Historical Museum is housed in the Baby family homestead. This neo-classic house built in 1811 now occupies several exhibitions that all depict the history of the area. Hiram Walker and Colio Wines offer plant tours with reservations made in advance. The city also possesses a number of attractive gardens and period buildings.

WINGHAM

Many who have read stories of the early settlement of Wingham wonder what prompted Edward Farley to settle in such a God-forsaken spot.

The story of Edward Farley begins in the mid-eighteen hundreds after the government laid out a town site at the junction of the north and south branches of the Maitland River, some forty miles north of Stratford. The new town plot was called Wingham.

In the spring of 1858, Farley and family left their home near Owen Sound. Their belongings went by boat to Collingwood. They travelled to Toronto on The Great Northern Railway and transferred to The Buffalo and Lake Huron Railway which took them to the end of the line in Stratford. At that point he hired freighters to haul his possessions the rest of the way to what is now Wingham, but the roads were in such poor shape, he was stranded in Blyth.

He hired four oxen and a wagon to take them to Bodmin in Morris Township. In those days Bodmin was a thriving hamlet on the Maitland River with a post office, mill, shops and a hotel. Here he constructed a raft to float their possessions down river.

Local legend has it that Farley, an intrepid Irishman, finally arrived at his destination on St. Patrick's Day.

The land on which the town plot of Wingham had been laid out proved to be low-lying marsh, later known officially as Lower Wingham, or among the pioneers, as "the frog pond".

Why had Farley decided to settle in such a place? No one will ever know.

He is not mentioned in the development of the area. His name was never used for anything except the hill where he built his log house. Years later the knoll where his home once stood was leveled to clear the way for a paved road.

In 1860, Peter Fisher arrived on horseback in Lower Wingham. He had been seeking a water privilege for flour and woollen mills. In Teeswater, then a small village, he was informed that a water privilege was for sale in Wingham. He proceeded to Zetland where he asked for directions to Wingham. No one there was aware of the existence of such a place. Undaunted, he headed east through the wilderness and eventually found the town plot and the location of the water privilege.

The first settler on the site of present-day Wingham was John Cornyn. He arrived with his three sons in 1859 and built the first public house in the vicinity. First known as the King William Hotel, it was replaced by the Queen's Hotel in later years.

By 1870, the London, Huron and Bruce Railway had arrived in Wingham. Until then, Wingham consisted of two hamlets, Lower Wingham and Upper Wingham and the railway spurred it on to become a very active business centre. Lower Wingham eventually disappeared.

In 1874, Wingham had a population of seven hundred and was incorporated as a village; three years later it was a town. There were eight hotels, six churches, and a new public school that could accommodate enrolment of four hundred.

Early in 1896, Wingham made headlines in the Toronto and American papers. The media created a picture of Wingham as a semi-barbarous hamlet known as the "Wingham Outrage".

It all began on the night of March 10, 1896, when a group of Wingham men met in a barn to discuss a problem concerning one of their neighbours, a Wingham businessman. They designed an attack - they blackened their faces, broke into his house and dragged him out into the cold clad only in a shirt. One man held a pistol to the head of the victim's son throughout the assault. The men finished the attack by tarring and feathering and then whipping him.

The next morning the son was advised to tell his father to leave town until tempers cooled. He caught the train to London where he died from exposure and blood poisoning in his feet that had been caused by freezing.

A bailiff from Goderich came to Wingham and arrested five men. A judge sentenced two men to three years in prison, two men to two years in prison and the fifth man was given six months.

Dr. Macdonald, a local member of parliament, contacted the Minister of Justice to see if the men could be paroled. The reason for the tarring and feathering was printed in the local newspaper for the first time. Apparently the victim was guilty of incest. Sir Oliver Mowat replied to Macdonald that Lynch law and Lynch Justice could not be tolerated. He would not consent to parole, but reduced the sentences of the four men to one year each.

Wingham, in the 1920's and 1930's, had a main street boulevard. Between the pavement and the sidewalk were utility poles and gasoline pumps. On the east side of the street was a "clear vision" gasoline pump, so called because the gasoline was always in view on the top of the stand and you could watch the level change as you were getting your tank filled. This pump was in front of Fry's Hudson-Essex Sales in the old Gracey building. Next door in the Shaw Block was the butcher shop and Dr. Margaret Calder's medical office. Next was the three-story Brunswick Hotel, with a large dome in the front above the entrance. Up the street was the Bell sign on the front of the telephone office. Across John Street, the Stone Block was just that, not plastered over as it is now, with the old entrance at the corner to the plumbing shop. In the background stood the town clock on the post office tower.

On the west side of the street was the Carter Bake Shop and Mrs. Cumming's Grocery, with a one-cent gum machine between them. Christie's Grocery, the drug store and Robertson's Garage followed. There were two gas pumps in front of the garage with two brands of gas, White Rose and British American.

Today to find a parking spot is a difficult chore; the hydro poles have disappeared behind the stores; the gas pumps no longer exist on the street; the Brunswick Hotel and the butcher shop have disappeared; there is no express office, no telephone operators. The Hudson, Essex and Studebaker cars have long since disappeared.

In 1935, Wingham was awarded a commercial radio license and W.T. (Doc) Cruikshanks began operating Station CKNX. Wingham at one time had the distinction of being the smallest town in Canada to have its own television station. By 1980 the population was 2,860 – small but with a very large pioneering spirit in evidence.

WOODSTOCK

The Woodstock Militia marching down the main street, c. 1860.

Who first founded Woodstock? Although most of the leg work during the early stages of development was done by his agent, Captain Andrew Drew, R.N., the actual credit has been given to Rear Admiral Henry Vansittart.

Upon his arrival in York from England, the Captain heard tales of Governor Simcoe's earlier attempts to establish military colonies in the western part of the province. In 1832, Drew was sent on behalf of the Admiral to purchase a tract of land which is now part of the eastern section of Woodstock. The Captain had the land divided into lots and had homes built for himself and for the Vansittarts. Governor Simcoe had already laid out a town plot in the western part of the site.

In 1834, the Admiral joined Drew and proceeded to construct a store and a tavern. He also saw to the financing of St. Paul's Church, which was built the same year. The church is one of the oldest landmarks to be found in Woodstock; it was consecrated by Bishop Mountain in 1838.

It wasn't long before other retired military officers and their families followed the Admiral and settled on his land. Among them were Colonel Light, Captain Graham, and Messrs. Hunter, Riddell, Deedes, Buller and Gibson. The presence of these distinguished officers and their ladies provided a gracious air to the new settlement. The newcomers chose the name Woodstock in honour of the Duke of Marlborough, whose estate of Blenheim Palace was near the village of Woodstock in Oxfordshire, England.

In 1835, a library and post office were established and the following year the General spearheaded the formation of the Oxford County Agricultural Society.

Woodstock was the second largest community in Oxford County by 1846 and in 1851, the year of incorporation as a village, the boundaries grew larger still. The town hall was erected in 1851- 52 and served as municipal offices, as a courthouse, as a lecture theatre, and as an opera house. This time also heralded the arrival of the Great Western Railway to Woodstock and it spurred on such growth that the village became incorporated as a town in 1857. Woodstock was incorporated as a city in 1901 and became the judicial centre for Oxford County.

The municipality grew by annexation when in 1964 and again in 1967 parts of West and Zorra East were added to the city. By 1980, Woodstock had a population of approximately 26,400. Development has brought a variety of industries to Woodstock and among their products are textiles, tubing, livestock, poultry feed, fire equipment, garden tools, agricultural and wood products.

Woodstock has a public library, a general hospital, a school of nursing and churches of various faiths. At one time there was a co-educational college known as Woodstock College that provided training in theology and the arts. It operated from 1860 to 1890 and then became a boys' preparatory school until it closed its doors in 1926. There are comprehensive educational facilities in Woodstock today including St. Joseph's Academy which finds its home in the house of Thomas Leopold "Carbide" Wilson who discovered acetylene.

You can see why Governor Simcoe and Admiral Vansittart, both of English origin liked the area of land surrounding Woodstock when you take a drive through Oxford County. Located on the Thames River, the countryside is generally rolling and its topography resembles that of the midland counties of England. The drumlin field around Woodstock is the largest of its kind in Western Ontario.

The city of Woodstock is a well-preserved community with many substantial houses dating from the mid-1800's. The Woodstock museum, located in the old town hall, features the restored council chambers of 1879 and a variety of exhibits depicting the colourful local history.

BIBLIOGRAPHY

Allan, Mrs. Roberta. History of Elora, Elora Women's Institute. Elora, 1982

Boyle, Terry. Under This Roof. Doubleday Canada Limited, 1980

Brown, Harman, Jeannere. Canada in North America 1800-1901. The Copp Clark Publishing Company Limited, Toronto, 1961

Craig, John. The Recent Past. Barrie, 1977

Ellis, Merrick Bernice. Travel Down A Storied Road. Cookstown, 1988

Leitch, Adelaide. The Visible Past, The Pictorial History of Simcoe County. 1967

Martin, Virgil. The Early History of Jacobstettels. St. Jacobs, 1979

Mifflin-Weeks, Mary; Mifflin, Ray. Harbour Lights Burlington Bay. The Boston Mills Press, Erin, 1989

Moyer, Bill. Kitchener, Yesterday Revisited. Windsor Publications Ltd, Burlington, 1979

Mika, Nick and Helma. Places in Ontario, Part One—A-E. Mika Publishing Company, Belleville, 1977

Mika, Nick and Helma. Places in Ontario, Part Two—F-M. Mika Publishing Company, Belleville, 1981

Mika, Nick and Helma. Places in Ontario, Part Three—N-Z. Mika Publishing Company, Belleville, 1983

Miller, Orlo. This Was London, Butternut Press Inc. Westport, Ontario, 1986

Roach, Al. All Our Memories, Part Two. Windsor, 1986

Robertson, J. Ross. The Diary of Mrs. John Graves Simcoe. Toronto, 1911

Robertson, Norman. History of the County of Bruce, fourth printing. Wiarton, 1988

Smith, Donald. Sacred Feathers. University of Toronto Press, Toronto, 1987

Tait, George. One Dominion Under the Name of Canada. The Ryerson Press, Toronto, 1963

PHOTO CREDITS

Author Photo: Edward Ufniak
All archival photographs are from Ontario Public Archives, with the following exceptions:
London Regional Art and Historical Museum: 89, 93
Alan Noon: 91
Public Archives Canada: 31, 55, 108, 118 (right), 132, 181
Simcoe County Archives: 6, 32, 34, 36, 184
Wellington County Museum Archives: 47, 198

Map of Western Ontario, showing the towns and cities described in this book.